MAP A

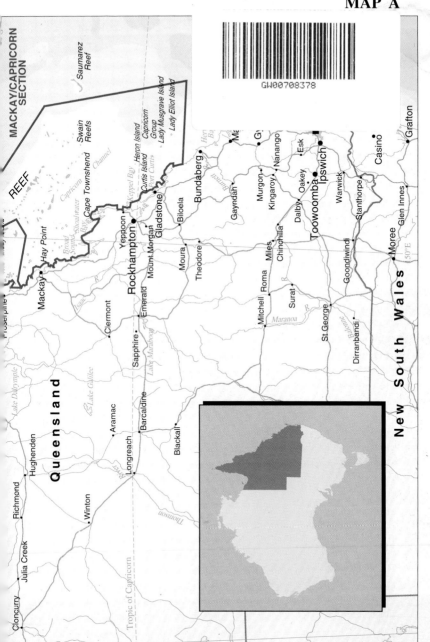

MACKAY/CAPRICORN SECTION

Saumarez Reef

Swain Reefs

REEF

Capricorn Channel

Heron Island
Capricorn Group
Lady Musgrave Island
Lady Elliot Island

Cape Townshend

Broad Sound
Shoalwater Bay

Keppel Bay
Curtis Island
Port Curtis

Hervey Bay

Hay Point

Mackay

Yeppoon
Rockhampton
Mount Morgan
Gladstone
Biloela

Bundaberg

Gayndah

Gympie

Murgon
Kingaroy
Nanango
Oakey

Esk

Ipswich
Toowoomba

Casino

Grafton

Warwick

Stanthorpe

Glen Innes

Clermont

Emerald
Sapphire

Moura

Theodore

Miles
Chinchilla

Dalby

Goondiwindi

Moree

Lake Dalrymple

Hughenden

Richmond

Julia Creek

Cloncurry

Queensland

Lake Galilee

Aramac

Barcaldine

Longreach

Winton

Blackall

Thomson

Lake Maraboon

Mitchell   Roma

Surat

Maranoa

St George

Dirranbandi

Balonne

New South Wales

Tropic of Capricorn

Isaac

Dawson

Isaac

50°E

Short Stay Guide

Australia's
Great Barrier Reef

Little Hills Press

Text ©Little Hills Press, February 2001
Photographs courtesy of Tourism Queensland ©Tourism Queensland
Maps by MAPgraphics ©Little Hills Press, 2001

Editor: Mark Truman
Cover Design by Artitude

Printed in Hong Kong

Australia's Great Barrier Reef
Short Stay Guide
ISBN 1 86315 146 X

Little Hills Press
Sydney, Australia
www.littlehills.com
info@littlehills.com

DISCLAIMER
Whilst all care has been taken by the publisher and authors to ensure that the
information is accurate and up to date, the publisher does not take responsibility for the
information published herein or the consequences of its use. The recommendations are
those of the writing team, and as things get better or worse, with places closing and
others opening, some elements in the book may be inaccurate when you arrive. Please
inform us of any discrepancies so that we can update in subsequent editions.

Little Hills and are registered trademarks of Little Hills Press Pty Ltd.

CONTENTS PAGE

Part Three: Appendix

Welcome to Australia's Great Barrier Reef

This magnificent region was included on the World Heritage List in 1981. Its clear, warm waters bustle with marine life and sustain amazing clusters of bright coral. Countless islands rise above the reef, breathtaking in their unique beauty and tranquil isolation.

Activities abound here in Queensland's north, from bushwalking through National Parks and rainforests, 4WD exploring, island camping, swimming, snorkelling, scuba diving, sailing, reef fishing, coral cruising, jetskiing, windsurfing and skydiving, to touring historic townships a little further inland. Or you can simply relax on perfect beaches beneath the swaying palms of this pristine paradise.

If you wish, travel by road from town to town and use this book to discover the best places to stay and dine and the attractions that each area has to offer. If you are pressed for time, make efficient and informed decisions about the type of islands that suit you, the cruises and tours that cater to your interests, and the landscapes to which you are drawn.

This guide book is designed to lead you through the best Australia's Great Barrier Reef has to offer.

Safe travelling. We hope your stay is enjoyable and memorable.

HOW TO USE THIS BOOK

Symbols

Throughout the text you will find that symbols have been used to denote the information that follows, whether it be an admission price, opening time, phone number or web address. This will aid you in locating the specific details you desire more quickly. Here is a list of the symbols used with an explanation of each:

> ℭ indicates a phone number
>
> ✪ indicates a price

⊙ indicates opening times

👁 indicates a web address

✎ indicates email

Goods and Services Tax

Perhaps the most significant development to affect the reading of this guide is the imposition of the nation-wide 10% GST, introduced on 1 July, 2000. The prices quoted in this book do not include the GST. It should also be kept in mind that many products are exempt from the tax, including basic food items.

Environmental Management Charge (EMC)

In April 1998, the Australian Government introduced an EMC for the Great Barrier Reef and environs. As a result, Tourist Operators must collect $4 from every visitor over the age of four who uses their services. Also known as the Reef Tax, the money raised through this scheme is used by the Great Barrier Reef Marine Park Authority for the purposes of the sustaining, protecting and managing the reef for the benefit of future generations.

Note that any prices for tourist services listed in this book do not include the EMC, so visitors should be aware of the extra fee.

Accommodation and Eating Out

In the Accommodation and Eating Out sections, we have tried to cater for a range of tastes and provide suggestions for your selection. The places mentioned are designed to give you a basis for comparison and to act at the very least as a starting point for the planning of your holiday. All budgets from lavish to limited have been considered and included. Note that accommodation is rarely cheap on the islands (unless you are camping) and it may be more feasible to use the coastal settlements as your springboard for day trips out to the Reef. The cities and towns offer far more competitive rates. As a general rule, the service at each listed establishment is typically efficient and the facilities satisfactory. With regard to eating out, remember that there are always cheaper meals available at fast food outlets and at the food courts of most shopping complexes. We have focused on listing only popular and recommendable restaurants. Again, the GST is excluded from any prices listed.

Layout

The chapters of this book are laid out in logical order, with places listed one after the other from north to south (Cape York down to Bundaberg). Information on how to get to each location caters for people travelling in either direction.

The content covers every aspect that a visitor requires to gain the most knowledge of a region with which they are unfamiliar. From entertainment to sport, to points of interest, to local transport, to tours and cruises, we have approached in detail every way a visitor might occupy his or her touring time, with the intention of helping to make the most of that limited time. The chapters and secondary headings are clear for your ease of use, and our comprehensive Index will assist you to locate your interests swiftly.

Telephone Number Listings

Most of the phone numbers listed in this book do not have the area or country codes preceding them. The reason for this is that both codes are standard and need mentioning only once. Here are the rules:

If you are calling Queensland from within Australia, but from another state, precede the eight-digit number with the (07) prefix, eg. dial 07 4055 1234.

If you are calling Queensland from another country, precede the area code with the (61) country code, leave out the 0 in the area code, then dial the eight-digit number, eg. dial 61 7 4055 1234.

Internet Information

For your convenience you will find at the end of this book a chapter listing transport and tourist information on the web.

PART ONE

Introduction

Introduction

AUSTRALIA: AN OVERVIEW

Australia is an island continent in the South Pacific Ocean. It is the smallest continent and the largest island in the world with a coastline of 19,650km. Its nearest neighbours are New Zealand and Papua New Guinea, while East Timor and Indonesia are a little further away, off the north-western coast.

The country has an area of 7,682,300 square kilometres and is divided into six states - New South Wales, Queensland, Victoria, Tasmania, South Australia and Western Australia - and two territories - Northern Territory and Australian Capital Territory.

The capital of Australia is Canberra in the Australian Capital Territory (ACT). The capital cities of the states are as follows:

New South Wales - Sydney
Victoria - Melbourne
Queensland - Brisbane
Tasmania - Hobart
South Australia - Adelaide
Western Australia - Perth
Northern Territory - Darwin

OVERSEAS VISITORS

Entry Regulations

All travellers to Australia need a valid passport, and visitors of all nationalities, except New Zealand, must obtain a visa before arrival. These are available at Australian Embassies, High Commissions and Consular offices listed in local telephone directories. No vaccinations are required.

Before you land you will be given immigration forms as well as Customs and Agriculture declarations. As a general rule you must declare all goods of plant or animal origin. Quarantine officers will inspect these items and return them to you if no disease or pest risk is involved. Even if they are not prohibited, some may need to be treated before being allowed entry.

Each incoming traveller over the age of 18 years is allowed duty free goods to the value of $400, plus 1125mL of liquor and 250g of tobacco products. These items must not be intended for commercial purposes and you must carry them with you through customs.

Exit Regulations

There is a Passenger Movement Charge or Departure Tax of $30 for everyone over the age of 12 years, but this is generally pre-paid with inclusion in the price of an airline ticket. People taking money out of the country, above the value of A$10,000 in Australian and/or foreign currency, must file a report with Customs. For more information on Customs or Quarantine Regulations, visit the following web sites:

👁www.aqis.gov.au for Quarantine
👁www.customs.gov.au for Customs

GST Refund

Overseas visitors qualify for a part refund of any GST they pay for items bought in Australia, if the total purchases made at any one

Introduction

business exceeds $300, and the purchases were made no more than 30 days before the date of departure. At the time of writing, the refund scheme involves presenting your claim to an established Customs booth at the Airport on the day of departure. The items on which you are allowed to claim back GST are only the hand-held items you intend to carry with you onto the plane. Present your documents to an officer for verification and you will then be directed to another booth where you will be given the refund to which you are entitled. If the total is less than $200 you can ask for the refund to be made in cash, otherwise it will be in the form of a mailed cheque or a credit arrangement. Foreign currency will also be accommodated in this transaction. Note that any general consumption purchases made within Australia (for example, hotel accommodation or meals) do not qualify for a refund claim.

Be aware that there will be no GST imposed on duty-free items sold in duty-free stores.

For further details and enquiries, phone the Australian Customs Information Line on ✆1300 363 263.

Embassies

Nearly seventy countries have diplomatic representation in Canberra. Some missions are called Embassies, and others who represent countries belonging to the Commonwealth, are called High Commissions. There are also Consuls in the State capitals, and their addresses can be found in the local White Pages telephone directory.

Following are the addresses of a few diplomatic missions in Canberra. The area code is (02).

New Zealand: Commonwealth Avenue, Canberra, ✆6270 4611.

Canada: Commonwealth Avenue, Canberra, ✆6270 4000.

Britain: Commonwealth Avenue, Canberra, ✆6270 6666.

USA: Moonah Place, Yarralumla, ✆6214 6600.

Singapore: Forster Crescent, Yarralumla, ✆6273 3944.

Japan: Empire Circuit, Yarralumla, ✆6273 3244.

Money

The Australian Currency is decimal, with the dollar as the basic unit. Notes come in a colourful array of $100, $50, $20, $10 and $5 denominations, with minted coins for lesser amounts - gold $1 and $2 coins, and silver 50c, 20c, 10c and 5c.

Currency exchange facilities are available at international airports, and most banks and large hotels.

The Australian dollar tends to fluctuate quite frequently, but approximate rates of exchange at time of writing, which really must be used as a guide only, are:

$$
\begin{array}{rcl}
NZ\$ & = & A\$0.82 \\
CAN\$ & = & A\$1.13 \\
UK£ & = & A\$2.60 \\
US\$ & = & A\$1.65 \\
S\$ & = & A\$0.96 \\
Baht & = & A\$0.04
\end{array}
$$

For the most accurate and up-to-date currency conversions, it is recommended that you use the simple and easy facility at ✆www.xe.net/ucc

Travellers cheques are the most convenient way of carrying money when travelling, and these can be exchanged at any bank, large hotels, and in large department stores. If you are intending to stay in Australia for any length of time, you might consider opening a bank account with automatic teller facilities. Automatic Teller Machines are widely available, both in the cities and in country towns, and most are open 24 hours a day. Different banks have different withdrawal limits, but it is generally about $1000 per day. All Australian banks operate this type of account.

GENERAL INFORMATION

Telephones

If you are calling any Sydney number from overseas, dial 61 for the country code and 2 for the area code, then the eight digit number.

Australia's recently revised area codes have simplified phone numbers across the country. Area codes now refer to states rather than districts. If calling from interstate, use the following prefix before any number you dial to:

New South Wales	- (02)
Australian Capital Territory	- (02)
Victoria	- (03)
Tasmania	- (03)
Queensland	- (07)
South Australia	- (08)
Western Australia	- (08)
Northern Territory	- (08)

Public telephones are easy to find in the cities and suburbs on street corners, in hotels, shops, cafes, and so on. A local call costs 40c from a phone box, but may be dearer from the privately leased phones outside shops. Emergency calls are free.

For international calls, you can dial direct to nearly 20 countries from almost any hotel, home, office or public phone in Australia. Simply dial 0011 + country code + area code + local number. Country Direct is the easiest way of making international telephone card and reverse charge (collect) calls. Upon dialling your Country Direct number, you are immediately put in touch with your own country's operator who will then connect the call. To find out your country's number ©1800 801 800 (free call).

Newspapers

Morning and afternoon newspapers are available everywhere, with each state having their own press, as well as selling the national paper

The Australian. There are also several local papers in city and suburban areas which have local news and advise on local events, such as *The Sydney Morning Herald* in Sydney and *The Age* in Melbourne.

Radio and Television

There is a national radio station and a national television channel, both of which are run by the Australian Broadcasting Commission (ABC). The capital cities have many AM and FM radio stations, and several free-to-air television channels. The television channels are: 2 (the national channel), 7 (commercial), 9 (commercial), 10 (comm-ercial) and 0 (SBS, which is government sponsored and has mostly foreign language programs, with English sub-titles). Regional areas broadcast programs on these networks, so their may be slight differences in programming (eg. *WIN* (9) in Wollongong and *Prime* (7) in Newcastle). Cable television is also available.

Post

Australia has an efficient postal service, and postcards sent by airmail to overseas countries cost $1. To send a letter by Air Mail (weighing up to 50g) to the Asia Pacific Zone costs $1 and to the Rest of the World, $1.50.

Time Zones

Australia is divided into three time zones: Australian   Eastern Standard Time, which covers Queensland, NSW, Victoria and Tasmania, is GMT plus 10 hours; Australian Central Standard Time, which covers South Australia and the Northern Territory, is GMT plus 9.5 hours; and Australian Western Standard Time, which covers Western Australia, is GMT plus 8 hours.

During summer, some of the states operate on daylight saving, putting their clocks ahead one hour on a designated Sunday morning in October, and back one hour on a Sunday in March. For NSW, Victoria and South Australia, it is the last Sunday in October and the first Sunday in March, but Tasmania remains on Summer Time until the end of March. Western Australia, Queensland and the Northern

Introduction

Territory do not have daylight saving, so at those times there are five different time zones in the country.

Credit Cards

American Express, Diners Club, Visa, Bank Card and MasterCard are widely accepted and usually signposted at participating retail outlets.

Electricity

Domestic electricity supply throughout Australia is 230-250 volts, AC 50 cycles. Standard three pin plugs are fitted to domestic appliances. 110v appliances, such as hairdryers and contact lens sterilisers, cannot be used without a transformer.

Videos

Australia uses the PAL system of videos. For the US market, tapes must be the NTSC system.

Internet General Information Sources

For general information on Australia, the best site to explore is ☜www.australia.com which is the offical web page of the Australian Tourist Commission.

For phone numbers nationwide, go to:

☜www.whitepages.com.au
☜www.yellowpages.com.au
☜www.colourpages.com.au

For additonal *Internet Information*, see the section at the back of the book.

Introduction

GREAT BARRIER REEF FACTS

AN OVERVIEW

The Great Barrier Reef extends 2030km from Breaksea Spit on the Queensland coast of Australia (south of the Tropic of Capricorn), to the coastal waters of New Guinea, making it the longest series of coral reefs and islands in the world. It consists of thousands of atolls, islands, shoals, reefs and coral formations that combine to form a barrier between the Pacific Ocean swells and the calmer coastal waters.

Scientists estimate that the Reef has grown from the seabed, involving billions of coral polyps over a period of around 500,000 years, and that the living coral continues this process today. The Reef has attracted a plethora of living organisms which interact with one another so closely that they and the Reef cannot be distinguished, and in fact the two are considered to be a single living organism.

When the Matthew Flinders expedition circumnavigated Australia in 1802, many previously unknown parts of its coastline were charted. In 1815 Charles Jeffreys sailed the entire length of the Queensland coast, within the boundaries of the Reef, and in 1819 Phillip King completed the task of charting the area. His report established that taking the route inside the reef was the quickest and safest way to sail along Australia's north-eastern coast.

CHARACTERISTICS

From the northern end, the Reef lies close to the coastline for about a thousand kilometres. Towards the southern end it veers away and breaks into a series of wide reefs that have proven to be shipping hazards in the past because of deceptively deep water between the shoals. In some places the outer edges of the reefs are less than 16km from the shore; in others they are as much as 320km.

The southern waters of the Reef are home to the reefs and bays of the **Bunker** and **Capricorn** groups, considered by some to be the most beautiful of the Reef's coral formations. Elsewhere, the coral and reef life are not in such profusion.

Heron Island, with an area of 17ha, lies on the Tropic of Capricorn, and is home to a Marine Biological Research Station. Heron, in common with the larger islands of the Reef, is a National Park, which is good news for the green turtles who come to lay their eggs each November, and the mutton birds and terns who nest on the island.

Great Keppel Island, off Yeppoon, and **Quoin**, in Port Curtis, are close to the coast and high and rocky. Further north are the **Percy Islands** and groups of similar islands that are virtually untouched.

The **Whitsunday Passage** is north of Mackay, and was founded and named by Captain Cook on Whitsunday 1770. The passage divides the **Cumberland Islands** from others nearer to the coast, including the resort islands of **Long**, **Brampton**, **Lindeman**, **Hamilton**, **South Molle**, **Whitsunday**, **Daydream** and **Hayman**. All these islands can be reached by plane and helicopter services from Mackay or Proserpine, a further 130km north. A cruise through the Whitsundays is high on the list of 'most popular holidays' for Australians as well as overseas visitors.

From Bowen, north of Proserpine, to Cairns, there are clusters of rocky islands, cays and coral reefs along the coast. The most accessible island is **Magnetic**, 8km from Townsville, then further north are **Great Palm**, **Orpheus**, **Hinchinbrook**, **Bedarra** and **Dunk**. With the exception of Great Palm Island, each has at least one resort and also other accommodation available.

Off-shore from Cairns are **Fitzroy** and **Green Islands**, with accommodation available on Green Island, as well as an underwater observatory, and a reef aquarium.

HISTORY

Australia's Aboriginal people not only knew of the existence of the Reef, they had large outrigger canoes that enabled them to travel to the islands and outer reefs. They moved their settlements up and down the coast for thousands of years before the coming of the Europeans.

Introduction

Sixteenth century maps include parts of the north and east coasts of Australia, but do not contain warnings of any hazards to shipping. It is known that Spanish, Chinese and Portuguese sailors were familiar with the Timor area and other parts to the north of Australia. For example, the 1606 expedition of Captain Torres in the caravel *San Pedrico* sailed through the strait that has been named in his honour. So it is possible that someone ventured further south, but there is no record of any one having done so.

Captain James Cook is the first person to record the existence of a reef as he sailed up the eastern coast of the continent. He first noticed shoals in the vicinity of Great Keppel Island, but he managed to continue north through the Whitsunday Passage, christening features and islands along the way. The *Endeavour* finally ran aground on a small reef near present day Cape Tribulation, and only expert seamanship enabled the vessel to limp more than 70km to the mouth of a river where repairs could be carried out. Today the river is called the Endeavour, and the settlement on its banks is Cooktown.

Two months later when the *Endeavour* was as ship-shape as possible, Cook decided to try for the open sea, but could not find a way through the natural barrier. He sailed north in search of a passage and reached Lizard Island, which he named because of its large population of these reptiles. Landing on the island, he and his botanist, Joseph Banks, climbed to its highest point and were able to see a break in the reef large enough to permit the passage of the *Endeavour*. On today's maps this is still known as Cook's Passage.

The first charts of the Reef were the work of another intrepid Englishman, Captain Matthew Flinders. He left Sydney on July 22, 1802, in the *Investigator*, and sailed up the north coast into the inner passage of the Reef. Using the technique of sending small boats ahead to sound the depths, Flinders charted a safe passage through the Reef, which is still known as Flinders' Passage. In fact, the soundings on his maps have been in use until quite recently. Incidentally, it was Flinders who gave the reef its name, Great Barrier Reef.

FLORA & FAUNA

When the Australian Government nominated the Great Barrier Reef for inclusion on the World Heritage List, it put forth the following:

- The Great Barrier Reef is by far the largest single collection of coral reefs in the world. Biologically the Great Barrier Reef supports the most diverse ecosystem known to man. Its enormous diversity is thought to reflect the maturity of an ecosystem which has evolved over millions of years on the north-east continental shelf of Australia.

- The Great Barrier Reef provides some of the most spectacular scenery on earth and is of exceptional natural beauty. The Great Barrier Reef provides a major feeding ground for large populations of the endangered species *Dugong dugon* and contains nesting grounds of world significance for the endangered turtle species of the green turtle (*Chelonia mydas*) and loggerhead turtle (*Caretta caretta*).

- The area nominated also meets the condition of integrity in that it includes the area of the sea adjacent to the Reef. The areas of this nomination contain many middens and other archaeological sites of Aboriginal or Torres Strait Islander origin. There are over 30 shipwrecks in the area, and on the islands, many of which are Queensland National Parks, there are ruins and operating light-houses which are of cultural and historical significance.

The Great Barrier Reef was inscribed on the World Heritage List on October 26, 1981.

Fauna

Dugongs are herbivorous marine mammals, who look a bit like fat dolphins but are actually related to the elephant. The early explorers, all of whom must have needed glasses, mistook the creatures for mermaids, in spite of their particularly unattractive snout.

As well as the turtles mentioned in the above nomination, the hawksbill turtle is found on the Reef. It is the scale of this turtle that is sold (in other countries) as "tortoise shell". Turtles are protected by law, and only Aborigines and Torres Strait Islanders are allowed to catch them as part of their cultural heritage. They are not permitted to sell any of their catch.

There are literally thousands of species of fish found living on the Reef, from small blennies who live on the bottom, to giant manta rays that can grow to seven metres across. In between there are fish of every size, shape and colour.

Other marine animals who make the waters of the Reef their home include sponges, worms, prawns, crabs, sea shells, sea-stars and sea squirts. Then, of course, there are the various coral polyps, which create living coral colonies. These are found in a variety of shapes and sizes that depend on how the individual polyps build their frames and bud off new polyps. Dead corals make up a reef, bound together by their own limestone and that of plant skeletons. Over thousands of years this reef of dead coral grows many metres thick, always covered with a coating of living coral. Coral spawning takes place in November/December each year, beginning a night or two after the full moon and lasting for about six nights. This event is unknown in any other part of the animal kingdom.

That brings us to the infamous Crown of Thorns Starfish (*Acanthaster planci*) - a predator that eats the coral polyps. Scientists have differing theories about this animal, which incidentally occurs in other areas of the Pacific, but they are keeping a close watch on their habitats and numbers.

Humpback whales, although not permanent residents of the reef, are annual visitors. Between July and October they can be found throughout much of the warm, shallow waters. Their smaller cousins, dolphins and porpoises, are regular visitors.

Land Animals

For obvious reasons the islands are not overrun with land species. However, some have colonies of flying foxes, or fruit bats, and others have a few wallabies, and possibly some bandicoots. Magnetic Island is home to some koalas and possums.

Birds

Many of the islands of the Reef are home to seabirds and wading birds, as well as over 150 other species. Seagulls, cormorants, pelicans and terns are some of the common species, but less common are shearwaters, petrels, boobies, tropicbirds and frigatebirds. The Great Barrier Reef Marine Park Authority produces a series of Reef Notes, and the one entitled *Seabirds* gives more information on the different species, and also advises how bird colonies should be approached to lessen the human impact.

Flora

There are sixty-five vegetated sand cays in the Barrier Reef region. Some of them have only one or two species of salt tolerant plants, others have up to forty species, including rainforest trees.

Some of the islands have mangrove forests, and some have varied plant life, it all depends on the richness of the soil, and the extent of rainfall.

Marine Stingers

There are a few marine "nasties" that also live in tropical waters. The chironex, also known as the *box jellyfish*, is present in the Rockhampton area from December to March, and in the Cairns area from late October to June. In other words, the further north, the longer the season. Stings from these creatures can be fatal. Not fatal, but still painful, are stings from *bluebottles* and *Pacific Man-o'War jelly blubbers*.

As an unbreakable rule: if you are told by a local resident or someone working at a resort, or if there is a sign on a beach that advises people not to swim - don't!

PROTECTING THE ENVIRONMENT

The Great Barrier Reef Marine Park is divided into sections, each of which has several zones.

- *General Use 'A' Zone* - line fishing and spear fishing, bait netting and gathering, crabbing and oyster gathering, diving, boating, trawling, and all reasonable uses are permitted.
- *General Use 'B' Zone* - reasonable uses are permitted, but no trawling.
- *Marine National Park 'A' Zone* - recreational use is permitted, ie fishing with one line and one hook is acceptable, but netting is prohibited; diving is fine.
- *Marine National Park 'B' Zone* - fishing is not permitted, but diving and photography are allowed.
- *Scientific Research Zone* - off-bounds for all except the scientific fraternity.
- *Preservation Zone* - completely off-limits except in cases of emergency.

Maps showing the various zones are readily available, and care should be taken to ensure that you do not enter a prohibited area.

Following is a list of things that visitors can do to play their part in protecting the environment.

The Reef

- Do not "souvenir" any animal or plant, whether dead or alive. This includes shells and corals.
- Always replace anything that you have moved.
- If in charge of a boat, always anchor with care. Use moorings when provided, or try to anchor in sand, making sure that the chain and rope will not foul coral.

Camping

- Use fireplaces where provided, not an open fire. Make sure the fire is out when you leave the campsite. Do not collect firewood from the reserve.
- It is preferable to use a fuel stove for cooking.
- Enquire about the availability of water at your chosen destination. It may be that you have to take drinking water with you.

- Use bins where provided, or take all rubbish when you leave.
- If toilets are not provided at camp sites, bury human wastes.
- Do not take domestic animals into National Parks and Forests.
- Do not use soap in freshwater lakes and streams.

Animals

- Do not disturb nesting seabirds.
- Keep to designated walking tracks through the forests.
- Do not feed silver gulls - their increased numbers are a threat to other birds.
- In summer, when the female turtle is crawling up the beach and digging her nest, make sure the beach is dark and quiet. She is easily disturbed and will return to the sea if frightened. Once she begins to lay her eggs she can be observed closely, and low lights can be used until she begins to return to the sea.
- When the baby turtles are hatching, the use of lights confuses them and they will head for the light instead of the sea, with disastrous results.

CLIMATE

Situated off the coast in the State of Queensland, the entire Great Barrier Reef is in the tropics, so it is never cold, varying instead between very warm and very hot.

Rockhampton, near the southernmost point of the Reef has January average temperatures of 31C (88F) max, 22C (72F) min. The July averages are 23C (73F) max, 9C (48F) min.

Cairns in the far north of Queensland has average January temperatures of 32C (90F) max, 24C (75F) min, and July temperatures of 25C (77F) max, 16C (61F) min.

In summer (December-February) the humidity is high, and if there is any chance of a cyclone, which can happen every few years, this is the season for it. Even if that doesn't eventuate, late summer is the wettest time of the year.

Consequently, the best time to visit the Reef area is from May to October.

POPULATION

The populated areas on the eastern coast of Queensland range from cities like Cairns, with around 70,000 residents, to small fishing villages with a couple of hundred people. The closest State Capital is Brisbane with around 1.2 million inhabitants.

HEALTH

Australia has excellent health services, but they do not come cheaply, especially if you are from overseas and are not covered by the Government-run Medicare. The necessity of having travel insurance that incorporates health insurance cannot be stressed enough. As someone once said about something else - don't leave home without it.

Whilst travelling in Queensland and on the Great Barrier Reef islands always wear a maximum protection sunscreen. Not only can a bad case of sunburn ruin your holiday, the effects of ultra violet rays can damage your skin irreparably.

Walking on the reef is a unique part of a Queensland holiday and is very enjoyable, but remember to wear sandshoes/runners, and treat any coral cuts carefully as they can easily lead to infection. A good method is to scrub the cut with a strong antiseptic till it bleeds (and hurts), thus ensuring that all foreign matter has been removed. If the cut should begin to swell, consult a doctor. Never dive or snorkel alone, and be careful of tides and currents.

TRAVEL INFORMATION

HOW TO GET TO AUSTRALIA

Unless visitors have plenty of time at their disposal the only way to get to Australia is to fly, and unless you come from New Zealand, it is going to be a long flight. Always consider a stop-over, on both flights if possible, but certainly on the flight home when you will be tired after your great holiday and subjected to jet lag. Somehow the excitement of what is in store seems to help with the outward flight.

Qantas, ℂ13 1313, Australia's major national carrier, has flights to Brisbane from Auckland, Christchurch, Wellington, Toronto, Vancouver, Honolulu, Singapore, Los Angeles, London, Seoul.

Qantas also has direct flights to Cairns from Hong Kong, Singapore, Taipei, Tokyo.

Air New Zealand, ℂ13 2476, has flights to Brisbane from Auckland, Christchurch, Wellington, Vancouver, Honolulu, Los Angeles.

British Airways, ℂ8904 8800, have flights to Brisbane from London.

Cathay Pacific, ℂ13 1747, has direct flights from Hong Kong to Brisbane and Cairns.

Singapore Airlines, ℂ13 1011, have direct flights to Brisbane.

United Airlines, ℂ13 1777, have flights to Brisbane from Los Angeles and San Francisco via Sydney.

HOW TO GET TO THE BARRIER REEF

People who have landed in Australia at one of the eastern capital cities then have a choice of how to get to the Reef - air, rail or road.

By Air

Qantas has daily flights from Sydney, Melbourne, Adelaide, Perth, Hobart, Darwin and Canberra to Brisbane.

They also have daily flights from Brisbane to Bundaberg, Cairns, Dunk Island, Great Keppel Island, Lizard Island, Mackay, Rockhampton, Toowoomba and Townsville, and daily except Saturday flights to Proserpine.

Ansett Australia have daily flights to Brisbane from Sydney, Melbourne, Adelaide, Perth, Hobart, Darwin and Canberra, although they are not all direct flights.

Ansett also have daily flights from Brisbane to Bundaberg, Cairns, Daydream Island, Hamilton Island, Long Island, Mackay, South Molle Island, Toowoomba, Townsville, and less frequent flights to Cooktown.

By Rail

The Sunlander leaves Brisbane on Tues, Thurs and Sat at 8.25am and travels through Rockhampton, Mackay, Townsville and Cairns.

The Queenslander leaves Brisbane on Sun at 8.25am and travels through Rockhampton, Mackay, Townsville and Cairns. It has first class carriages.

The Spirit of the Tropics leaves Brisbane on Wed and Sun at 8.25am and travels through Rockhampton, Mackay, Townsville and Cairns. It has economy class carriages.

The Spirit of Capricorn leaves Brisbane on Sat at 7.30am and travels through Maryborough, Bundaberg, Gladstone and Rockhampton.

The new *Tilt Train* is a high speed daily service that runs the same route as the Spirit of Capricorn and significantly reduces the travel time.

Queensland Rail Traveltrain can be contacted on ✆13 2232.

More information on train travel is found in the chapters on the various destinations.

By Bus

McCafferty's, ✆13 1499, and **Greyhound Pioneer**, ✆13 2030, are the main coach companies that operate in Australia's eastern states, so it is possible to travel with them Melbourne-Sydney-Brisbane-Cairns and points in between. But you would have to be a dedicated coach traveller to undertake the long hike from Melbourne to Cairns, or even from Sydney to Cairns - still it is a lot cheaper than air or rail travel. The distances are listed in the following section.

Introduction

By Road

If you are considering driving to Far North Queensland, it is a good idea to check out the distances involved.

Melbourne-Sydney via the Hume Highway - 875km; via the Princes Highway - 1058km; via the Olympic Way - 961km; via Cann River/Cooma/Canberra - 1038km.

Sydney-Brisbane via the Pacific Highway - 1000km; via the New England Highway - 1033km.

Brisbane-Rockhampton via the Bruce Highway - 670km; via Esk and Biloela - 758km.

Rockhampton-Cairns - 1136km.

Brisbane-Mackay via the Bruce Highway - 1020km

Mackay-Proserpine via the Bruce Highway - 127km

Mackay-Cairns - 779km.

Brisbane-Townsville via the Bruce Highway - 1433km.

Brisbane-Cairns via the Bruce Highway - 1799km.

ACCOMMODATION

On the mainland there is a wide choice of accommodation from 5-star hotels to camping areas. On the islands the choice is not so wide; it is usually between a resort hotel and camping, with nothing in between. And not all the islands have camping facilities. Full information on each island's available accommodation is found in the appropriate section of this book.

LOCAL TRANSPORT

Transport to the Reef and the island resorts from the various coastal cities and towns will be covered in detail in each of the chapters of this book.

FOOD & DRINK

Obviously seafood is going to feature largely on any north Queensland menu, as will tropical fruit. In the section on each city you will find a list of restaurants and their specialty.

Introduction

Included in the information on each island are details of the meal arrangements for the resorts. Some of the accommodation costs include meals, others don't.

Restaurants in Australia are either Licensed or BYO, although some can be both. Without going into the licensing laws of why this is so, here is a short explanation of how it will affect the diner.

A *licensed restaurant* has a wine list, and can provide beer, mixed drinks, ports, liqueurs, etc. Patrons are not allowed to provide their own drinks. A *BYO restaurant* does not have a licence to provide alcohol, so you Bring Your Own wine or beer or whatever. Glasses are provided, and a corkage fee (for opening the bottles!) may be charged, which can be per person or per bottle depending on the whim of the proprietor.

Some restaurants that do have a licence will allow you to bring your own wine (which works out cheaper), but you are not permitted to bring your own beer or spirits.

Liquor stores in Australia are called "bottle shops", and they are found everywhere.

Queensland has two main beer brands - XXXX (Fourex) and Powers, but beers from the other states, such as Tooheys, VB, Fosters and Cascade, are also found in the north.

Australian wines will also feature on all wine lists, and should be sampled by the overseas visitor. There are several extremely good wine growing areas in the country - Barossa Valley, Hunter Valley, Yarra Valley and Margaret River, to name a few.

SHOPPING

All the resort islands have stores that stock the basics of living, such as shampoo, soap, toothbrushes and toothpaste, etc, and there are usually boutiques and souvenir outlets as well. In the boutiques there is usually a good selection of sports wear, swimming costumes (locally called cozzies), board shorts, etc, but they are not exactly inexpensive.

The towns and cities on the mainland have shops and shopping centre and the usual ☉opening hours are Mon-Fri 9.30am-5.30pm (until 9pm on either Thurs or Fri) and Sat 9.30am-4pm. In the tourist areas the shops are usually open every day and for longer hours.

Toy kangaroos and koalas are high on everyone's shopping list, and are available everywhere. Everything Aboriginal is popular and items are found in all centres. The most sought after articles, though, are opals.

When buying opals there are a few terms you should be familiar with:

Solid Opal - this is the most valuable, and good for investment purposes. The more colourful and complete, the greater its value.

Doublet - this is slices of opal glued together, and is of medium value. It has no investment value.

Triples - this is slices of opal covered with quartz, perspex or glass, and is the least expensive. It has no investment value.

If your pocket can't stretch as far as a solid opal, but you still would like a piece of opal jewellery, remember that anything that is glued can come unstuck, and that condensation can form under perspex or glass. The less expensive types of opal are not suitable for rings, unless you are going to remember to take it off every time you wash your hands.

Australia produces more than 90% of the world's opals, and the three main areas where they are found are: Lightning Ridge, which produces the Black Opal; Quilpie, where the Queensland Bounder Opal originates; and Coober Pedy, which has the White or Milk Opal.

VISITOR INFORMATION

Every town has an information office but in the small towns it may be part of another shop, so just keep an eye out for a large 'i' sign, usually in white, blue or yellow.

Some road conditions in Far North Queensland vary frequently with seasonal rains and may become inaccessible or 4WD only overnight. To keep up to date with road conditions, two websites worth checking are ☞www.gulf-savannah.com.au and ☞www.racq.com.au Following is a list of details for various departments and organisations that dispense tourist information on the Great Barrier Reef area.

Australian Tourist Commission. 80 William Street, Woolloomooloo, Sydney, ☏1300 361 650. ☞www.australia.com

Tourism Queensland. 123 Eagle Street, Brisbane, ☏(07) 3406 5400. ☞www.qttc.com.au

Naturally Queensland. 160 Ann Street, Brisbane. ☏(07) 3227 8187

Environmental Protection Agency. 288 Edward Street, Brisbane. ☏(07) 3224 5641. ☞www.env.qld.gov.au

Great Barrier Reef Marine Park Authority. Flinders Street, Townsville, ☏(07) 4750 0700. ☞www.gbrmpa.gov.au

Queensland Government. ☏1800 803 788. ☞www.qld.gov.au

Youth Hostels Association of Queensland. 154 Roma Street, Brisbane, ☏(07) 3236 1680.

Youth Hostels Association of Australia. 422 Kent Street, Sydney, ☏9261 1111. ☞www.yha.com.au

The Queensland National Parks and Wildife Service (QNP&WS) controls most of the Great Barrier Reef Islands, and issues the necessary comping permits for them. Their regional office addresses are:

Brisbane. 160 Anne Street, Brisbane, ☏3227 8187.

Cairns (Northern Regional Office). 17-19 Sheridan Street, Cairns, ☏4052 3092.

Cairns District. Moffatt Street, Cairns, ☏4053 4533.

Cooktown District Office. Charlotte Street, Cooktown, ☏4069 5777.

Emerald District Office. 99 Hospital Road, Emerald, ℘4982 4555.

Gladstone District Office. 136 Goondoon Street, Gladstone, ℘4972 6055.

Innisfail District Office. 27-29 Owen Street, ℘4061 4291.

Longreach District Office. Landsborough Highway, Longreach, ℘4658 1761.

Mackay District Office. Corner Wood & River Streets, Mackay, ℘4951 8788.

Mossman District Office. Johnston Road, Mossman, ℘4098 2188.

Rockhampton (Central Region Office). Corner Yeppoon & Norman Roads, North Rockhampton, ℘4936 0511.

Townsville District Office. Marlow Street, Pallarenda, ℘4722 5388.

Whitsunday District Office. Corner Mandalay Road, Shute Harbour Road, Jubilee Pocket, Airlie Beach, ℘4946 7022.

QNP&WS also publish leaflets on most of the islands setting out the walking tracks and camping grounds, if any.

PART TWO

Great Barrier Reef

CAPE YORK TO CAIRNS

CAPE YORK

Map A

LOCATION AND CHARACTERISTICS

This remote mainland spur is Australia's northernmost tip, 2753km north of Brisbane. Like an outstretched finger the peninsula points towards the south coast of Papua New Guinea, just over 100km away on the other side of the Torres Strait. The Jardine National Park hugs the eastern portion of the Peninsula about 50km south of the Cape.

HOW TO GET THERE

By Air

Sunstate, ℰ13 1313, fly to Thursday Island, which is a short distance north-west of Cape York.

Flight West make trips to Bamaga, ℰ1300 130 092.

Ansett fly to Weipa, ℰ13 1300.

Cape York Air Services, ℰ4035 9399, operate out of Cairns Airport.

By Coach

Coral Coaches travel only as far north as Weipa, ℰ4031 7577.

By Car

From Cairns, the most direct route is by 4WD only via the Peninsula Development Road which cuts through the eastern side of the peninsula to Cape York. The journey is 861km on the direct route and 1062km if you weave through the National Parks. Road conditions vary with each Wet season, so it is essential that you check current road integrity with the Visitor Information Centre in Cairns, ✆4031 4355, or visit the relevant web pages listed in the *Tourist Information* chapter.

VISITOR INFORMATION

For a preliminary taste, the web pages to explore are ☞www.tnq.org.au and ☞www.visitcapeyork.com

Additional information can be obtained from the Cooktown Tourism Association, ✆4069 6100 or ✆1800 001 770. Their email address is ✉info@cooktownau.com

ACCOMMODATION AND SERVICES

Accommodation is varied but limited. Here are a few examples:

The *Pajinka Wilderness Lodge* is only 400m south of Cape York, ✆4031 3988. They have 24 units, resort facilities, a licensed restaurant and a pool - ✪$460-500 for two, for a three night minimum stay with all meals included.

You can camp in Seisia, 30km south of the Cape, at the *Seisia Village Campground*, Koroba Road, ✆4069 3243. It has 42 powered sites, a barbecue and an unlicensed restaurant open Mon-Sat - ✪$17 a double per night.

If neither of the above appeals, try the *Seisa Seaview Lodge*, also in Koroba Road, ✆4069 3243. It has 6 lodges, good facilities, an unlicensed restaurant, horse riding and a pool - ✪$350 a double per night.

POINTS OF INTEREST

Crocodile farming at the **Edward River Aboriginal Mission**, ✆4060 4177; pearl farming; black boar hunting; barramundi fishing, ✆4031 3988;

Swamp area, Cape York Peninsula

Cairns

and Aboriginal Corroborees at **Bamaga Mission**, are just a few of the unique attractions Cape York has to offer.

TOURS AND CRUISES

Last Frontier Safaris offer 1, 2 or 4 day wild pig hunts, so if this appeals to you, ✆4098 8264.

Several cruises sailing to Cape York and the Torres Strait are available, and this is probably the best way to visit this remote region if you are not the rugged, adventurous type.

Kangaroo Explorer Cruises, 2 Reservoir Road, Manunda, ✆4032 4000, sail from Cairns to Thursday Island, or vice versa, and offer 4-7 day cruises starting from ✪$984 including airfares to departure points and all meals.

In Cape York, the Pajinka Wilderness Lodge runs a number of tours, *Pajinka Pastimes*, which include 4WD safaris, fishing trips, bridwatching, wilderness walks and self-guided tours, ranging from ✪$15 to $60, ✆4031 3988.

From Cairns, *Quinkan Country Adventures*, 13 Shields Street, Cairns, ©4051 4777, operate tours to Aboriginal Rock Art sites in the Laura River Valley.

LIZARD ISLAND

Map A

LOCATION AND CHARACTERISTICS

With an international reputation as the place for big game fishing, Lizard Island is 97km (60 miles) north-east of Cooktown and is basically a 1000ha National Park boasting pristine natural beauty. It has an area of 21 sq km, and is the most northerly of the Barrier Reef resort islands. It is 240km from Cairns, but close to the outer Barrier Reef, and has 23 beaches that are good for swimming and snorkelling.

Captain Cook and Dr Joseph Banks landed on Lizard Island, after they had repaired the *Endeavour* at what is now Cooktown. They named it after the many large lizards they found there.

Shell middens found around the island testify to the fact that Aborigines had made it their home, and it is thought that parts of the island had some sacred meaning for them. This is given as the possible reason for the tragedy that occurred in the early 1880s. Robert and Mary Watson lived on the island and collected beche-de-mer (sea slugs), a Chinese delicacy. Robert left Mary and her baby in the company of two Chinese servants while he went off in search of new fishing grounds. Whilst he was away some Aborigines arrived on the island and killed one servant and wounded the other. Mary decided to leave the island, so she loaded the baby and the remaining servant into an iron tank and set off for the mainland. They never made it, and their bodies were discovered some months later on one of the Howick islands.

It is thought that inadvertently the Watsons may have interfered with an Aboriginal sacred site, thus causing the attack. The ruins of the Watson's house can still be seen, near the top of Cook's Look.

Lizard has over 1000ha of National Park, and some good walks. The climb to the top of Cook's Look is the most popular, and is well signposted, and from the Resort it is a short walk to the ruins of the Watson's house. The waters around the island are home to coral reefs and countless tropical fish, including the renowned Black Marlin. From August to November it attracts fishermen worldwide.

HOW TO GET THERE

The Island is very remote and exclusive, with access only via a scenic air one-hour flight from Cairns Airport. You can make arrangements when booking accommodation.

There are no regular ferry or boat services to Lizard Island, but it is included as a destination in some of the cruises run by Captain Cook Cruises, ©4031 4433.

VISITOR INFORMATION

You can explore the website at ☞www.lizardislandresort.com or email them at ✎visitors@greatbarrierreef.aus.net

The resort itself has all the facilities and information you require, so it is best to contact them directly with any queries.

ACCOMMODATION AND SERVICES

Accommodation is available in 40 well-appointed units facing the beach at the *Lizard Island Resort*, ©4060 3999. Tariffs start from ✪$540 twin share per person per night in the Anchor Bay Rooms, to $800 for the Premium Sunset Point Villas. Enquire also about package deals on offer at the time of your trip.

The room facilities consist of a private bathroom, refrigerator, mini-bar, air-conditioning, IDD/STD telephone, ironing facilities, daily cleaning service, writing desk and private verandah. The deluxe suites have a separate living area.

The above rates include all meals and free use of snorkelling gear, water skiing, tennis, surf skis, windsurfers, catamarans, basic fishing gear and outboard dinghies. Not included in the rates are game fishing boats and dive facilities.

Cairns

The standard and array of food in the restaurant is excellent, and the cost is included in the room tariff.

Note that children under 6 years of age are not catered for, but alternative arrangements may be made at the resort's discretion.

Camping is also available at Watson's Bay, by application and with a permit. Facilities include toilets, drinking water, barbecues and picnic tables. Contact the National Parks and Wildlife Service in Cairns, ©4052 3096, for more information.

POINTS OF INTEREST

The resort has a swimming pool, tennis court, a club-like lounge, a boutique, a small shop and a bar with a recorded history of the island's biggest catches.

The focus, however, is on getting wet, and there is a superb coral lagoon, shady white beaches (24 in total), good scuba diving areas, boating facilities and fishing opportunites. Available are paddle skis, outboard dinghies, catamarans, sailboards, snorkelling equipment, Outer Barrier Reef trips, eco tours, basic fishing gear, glass-bottom boat trips, scuba diving/training, waterskiis, boats and game fishing charters.

Aerial view of Lizard Island

DIVING

Some believe that Lizard Island has the best diving along the Great Barrier Reef, and in fact it is surrounded by excellent coral reefs.

The Ribbon Reefs lie only a 20 minute boat ride from the island. These are comprised of a string of ten coral ramparts that support an immense undersea world of living coral and sea animals, and the most spectacular underwater scenery. All the Ribbon Reefs are great, but following are a few highlights:

The Code Hole is world renowned and very popular. It is at the northern tip of Reef No. 10, and divers can hand feed giant Potato Cod, some over 2.5m in length.

Pixie Pinnacle is a coral bommie on the southern end of Reef No. 10. Here divers will find species of pelagic fish, black coral, and a host of tropical fish.

Dynamite Pass is a narrow area of water just north of Ribbon Reef No. 10. the depths range is from 4m to 40m below the surface, but visibility is about 30m and there is plenty to see.

Detached Reefs are located in the Coral Sea half-way between Cooktown and Cape York. Both reefs extend from a metre or so under the surface to the seabed some 500m below. This is sheer wall diving at its best with visibility extending more than 40m. Expect to see giant sponges, sea whips, Angelfish, Clownfish, Manta Rays, sharks and varieties of coral.

COOKTOWN

Map B
Population 1300

LOCATION AND CHARACTERISTICS

Cooktown is 246km north of Cairns. Its close proximity to Aboriginal culture, diverse wildlife, rainforests, unique land formations and extensive surrounding savannah, means that it can be described as the geographical intersection of Reef and Outback. The town is clustered on the banks of the scenic Endeavour River.

Cooktown is etched in history, drawn from the early days of its Aboriginal inhabitants, to Captain Cook's forced landing, to gold rush times and the adventures of subsequent pioneers and explorers.

HOW TO GET THERE

By Air

A flight to Cooktown takes just over half an hour from Cairns Airport. Ansett runs this service, ✆13 1300, as does Transtate, ✆13 1528.

By Coach

Coral Coaches run from Cairns as far north as Cooktown, ✆4031 7577.

By Car

From Cairns there are two options:

The direct route which follows the Bruce Highway (becomes the Captain Cook Highway out of Cairns) towards Mossman and Daintree, then turns right onto the signposted coastal road that passes Wujal Wujal, Rossville and Helensvale to Cooktown. Note that between Cape Tribulation and Helensvale the road is recommended for 4WD vehicles only.

Or you can take the winding inland route along part of the Peninsula Development Road, then turn right at Lakesland onto the connecting road which joins the coast road just north of Helenvale, then continue directly to Cooktown.

VISITOR INFORMATION

The Cooktown Tourism Association can be contacted on ✆4069 6100 or ✆1800 001 770. They have a website at ☛www.cooktownau.com and their email address is ✎info@cooktownau.com

ACCOMMODATION AND SERVICES

There are sufficient motels, guest houses and caravan parks to accommodate a short stay. Following is a list of suggestions to give you an idea of what is on offer, with prices for a double room per night.

The Sovereign Resort, cnr Charlotte & Green Streets, ©4069 5400. 26 rooms, 3 suites, licensed restaurant, pool - ✪$112-122.

Seagrens Inn, 12 Charlotte Street, ©4069 5357. 7 units, licensed restaurant, pool, wonderful beach and river views - ✪$40-60.

Milkwood Lodge Rainforest Cabins, Annan Road, ©4069 5007. 6 cabins, good facilities - ✪$80.

Caravan Park

Cooktown Tropical Breeze Caravan Park, cnr Charlotte Street & McIvor Road, ©4069 5417. 45 sites, barbecue and pool - ✪$15 powered sites, $49 cabins.

There is a **Youth Hostel** on the corner of Boundary and Charlotte Streets, *Pam's Place*, ©4069 5166. It has 13 twin share rooms at ✪$20 per person per night.

Eating Out

If you plan to dine out, the *Burragi Floating Restaurant*, in Webber Esplanade, is recommended, ©4069 5956.

POINTS OF INTEREST

Apart from the picturesque surrounds, it is worth exploring the historical buildings in Cooktown, including the old Post Office, Westpac Bank and the Sovereign Hotel. The **James Cook Historical Museum** is in Helen Street, ©4069 5386. Cook's Monument, The Cannon, Grassy Hill and the Chinese Graveyard are additonal points of interest.

Cooktown Tours, ©4069 5125, will take you by coach on a two-hour guided historical tour of the city for ✪$16 adults, $10 children, departing at 9am. Additional tours to nearby regions of natural or cultural interest are available:

Black Mountains & Lion's Den Tour, 4hrs, 9am departure, ✪$45 adults, $20 children.

Elim Beach and Coloured Sands, 5hrs, 9am departure, ✪$75 adults, $50 children.

Laura Aboriginal Rock Art Site & Lakefield National Park, 8hrs, 9am departure, ✪$100 adults, $70 children.

You can explore the coastal waters with *Cooktown Reef Charters*, ✆4069 5519.

DAINTREE AND CAPE TRIBULATION

Map B

LOCATION AND CHARACTERISTICS

25km (16 miles) north of Mossman and about 146km (92 miles) south of Cooktown lies the township of Daintree, nestled in the heart of the Daintree River catchment basin, surrounded entirely by the rainforest-clad McDowall Ranges. The Daintree National Park lies to the west and Cape Tribulation National Park to the east; both have flourished largely unspoilt for millions of years. A World Heritage listing now ensures the continued preservation of this 17,000ha region.

The area has an abundance of native plant-life, birds and exotic tropical butterflies. Australia's pre-historic reptile, the estuarine crocodile, can be seen lurking in the mangrove-lined creeks and tributaries of the Daintree River.

Cape Tribulation, where the rainforest meets the reef, is an increasingly popular tourist area for both camping and day visits. Crystal clear creeks and forests festooned with creepers and vines, palm trees, orchids, butterflies and cassowaries, are part of the Cape Tribulation experience in one of the country's finest rainforest areas.

There are several resorts, hostels and camping grounds.

The atmosphere is relaxed and 'alternative' in this tropical rainforest retreat. It is a very popular haven for backpackers.

HOW TO GET THERE

By Air

Daintree Air Services, ✆4034 9300, operate from Cairns. In Cape Tribulation there is an airport at Cow Bay, serviced by Hinterland Aviation, ✆4035 9323.

By Bus

Coral Coaches, ✆4031 7577, can take you to Daintree for ✪$30 one way.

By Road

From Cairns, simply follow the Bruce Highway north until it terminates at Daintree. Coming south from Cooktown, take the coastal road until it connects (and ends) with the Bruce Highway, then travel in a north-westerly direction for about 10km (6 miles) along the highway to Daintree. A vehicle ferry will take you across the Daintree River into Cape Tribulation.

It should be noted that caution must be exercised if driving a conventional vehicle, even one with high clearance, and during and after rain a 4WD vehicle is essential. The 32km narrow, unsealed Cape Tribulation/Bloomfield Road is recommended for 4WD only, and towing caravans should not be attempted.

VISITOR INFORMATION

The Daintree Tourist Information Centre is in 5 Stewart Street, ✆4098 6120. The Great Barrier Reef website has a section on Daintree at ☜www.greatbarrierreef.aus.net as does Tourism Tropical North Queensland at ☜www.tnq.org.au

ACCOMMODATION AND SERVICES

Accommodation is not abundant in the Daintree area, so it is advisable to book well in advance. Prices are for a double room per night.

Daintree Eco Lodge, Daintree Road, Daintree, ✆4098 6100. 30 units, licensed restaurant, heated pool - ✪$315-330.

Bloomfield Wilderness Lodge, Weary Bay, Daintree National Park, ✆4035 9166. 16 cabins, licensed restaurant, barbecue, pool, extensive package deals included in tariff, guided rainforest walks, Bloomfield River Cruise, all meals - ✪$60.

There are also camping facilities for $18 per double per night.

Daintree Manor, 27 Forest Creek Road, North Daintree, ✆4090 7041. 3 rooms, basic facilities - ✪$65-85.

Caravan Park

Daintree Riverview Caravan Park, 2 Stewart Street, ✆4098 6119. 26 sites, basic facilities - ✪$15 powered sites, $35 on-site vans.

Pilgrim Sands Holiday Park, Cape Tribulation, ✆4098 0030. 20 sites, limited facilities - powered sites ✪$15, cabins $57.

There is a **Youth Hostel** at Cape Tribulation, *Crocodylus Village*, Lot 5, Buchanan Creek Road, Cow Bay, ✆4098 9166. There are 8 twin share rooms at ✪$33 per person per night.

Eating Out

If you plan to eat out, a selection of restaurants includes the *Big Barrumundi Barbecue Garden*, 12 Stewart Street, ✆4098 6186; *Daintree Village*, 3 Stewart Street, ✆4098 6173; and *Jacanas*, 1 Stewart Street, ✆4098 6146.

POINTS OF INTEREST

The township has art and craft centres, and the **Daintree Timber Museum & Gallery**, 12 Stewart Drive, ✆4098 6166. The real attraction, however, is the National Park itself.

Given the majesty quality of the natural environment, the emphasis here is on eco-touring.

Several cruises operate on the Daintree River offering passengers a leisurely tour observing the beauty of the river and rainforest, and enjoying morning or afternoon tea. A few available are:

Daintree Dancer Sailing and River Cruises, Daintree Public Jetty, ✆4098 7960;

Daintree Lady Cruise, 13-15 Osborne Street, ✆4098 6138;

Electric Boat Cruises, Daintree Road, ✆4098 6103;

Daintree Rainforest River Train, Bailey Creek Road, ✆4090 7676.

There is a *Daintree Wildlife Safari* for the more adventurous explorers. They are located at 12 Stewart Street, ✆4098 6125.

Adventure Connections, Clifton Beach, ✆4059 1599, operate small tours that are designed to foster education and appreciation of the natural environment and its wildlife. They are run by people with botanical and zoological backgrounds who know what they are talking about. Prices start from ✪$105 per person. Nocturnal tours are also conducted for those who are interested.

The *Daintree River Ferry*, ✆4098 7788, which operates daily, takes visitors into the world of wilderness and rainforest at Cape Tribulation and beyond.

The famous **"bouncing stones"** are just north of Thornton's Beach.

MOSSMAN

Map B
Population 1850

LOCATION AND CHARACTERISTICS

171km south of Cooktown and only 20km (12 miles) north of Port Douglas, Mossman is in the heart of the Mossman Valley. It is a sugar town surrounded by green mountains (highest is Mt Demi, 1159m-3802 ft) and fields of sugar cane. Mossman is fast becoming well-known as a centre for exotic tropical fruit growing, and a number of farms conduct tours and offer their products for sale.

HOW TO GET THERE

By Air

Port Douglas has an airport, from which bus transfers can be arranged to Mossman. The Visitor Information Centre will assist you with arrangements, ✆4099 5599.

By Bus

Coral Coaches, ✆4098 2600, stop at Mossman on their Daintree route from Cairns.

By Road

The Bruce Highway passes through Mossman, about 75km north of Cairns.

VISITOR INFORMATION

The Queensland National Parks and Wildlife Service has a branch at Mt Demi Plaza, on the corner of Front and Johnston Streets, ©4098 2188. They can assist you with local details and it should be your first stop if you wish to explore this area.

For more information, contact the Visitor Information Centre in Port Douglas (*see separate listing*).

ACCOMMODATION AND SERVICES

Here is a selection of accommodation. Prices are for a double room per night.

Demi View, 41 Front Street, ©4098 1277. 12 units, licensed restaurant, undercover parking, pool - ✪$60-65.

Silky Oaks Lodge, Finlayvale Road, Mossman River, ©4098 1666. 60 chalets, licensed restaurant, guided bushwalks, tennis, pool, breakfast included - ✪$380.

Caravan Park

Mossman Bicentennial Caravan Park, Foxton Avenue, ©4098 1922. 43 sites, barbecue, standard facilities - powered sites ✪$17, on-site vans $25.

Eating Out

Three restaurants you might like to try are: *Chung Tai Chinese*, cnr Front Street & Johnston Road, ©4098 1102; *Jack High Bistro*, 6 Johnstone Road, ©4098 3166; and *Mojo's* 41 Front Street, ©4098 1202.

POINTS OF INTEREST

The business centre of the Douglas Shire, Mossman has wide tree-lined streets, colourful gardens and a large sugar mill. Guided tours of the **Mossman Sugar Mill**, Mill Site, ©4098 1400, are conducted during the cane crushing season (June to December).

Australian Wilderness Safaris operate out of Finlayvale Road, Mossman, ℂ4098 1766.

A few minutes' drive from the township, a sealed road leads to the **Mossman Gorge** in Daintree National Park. This is a wilderness area of 56,000ha (138,320 acres), with crystal clear running streams, waterfalls, walking tracks through towering rainforest, barbecue picnic sites and a unique suspension bridge over a steep ravine.

PORT DOUGLAS

Map B
Population 1400

LOCATION AND CHARACTERISTICS

The 83km (52 miles) drive north from Cairns to Port Douglas covers some of the most spectacular coastal strips and beaches in Australia. The Captain Cook Highway is wedged between towering, lush forest-covered mountains and the Coral Sea.

Situated 6km east of the highway, Port Douglas is one of the closest towns to the Great Barrier Reef. It has all the charm of a fishing port tastefully combined with modern tourism facilities.

Low Island, off Port Douglas

The township was settled in 1877 as the main port for the Palmer River goldfields, and today it is a popular departure point for professional and amateur fishermen, for trips to the outer reef and islands, and for scuba diving and aquatic sports.

HOW TO GET THERE

By Air

Sunlover Helicopters have transfer flights from Cairns Airport on arrangement, ✆4035 9669. For details on Port Douglas airport services, make enquiries at the Information Centre, ✆4099 5599.

By Coach

Coral Coaches, ✆4099 5351, have a service to Port Douglas for ✪$22 one-way. Sun Palm Express, ✆4099 4992, offer a return fare for $55.

By Road

Port Douglas is a short distance towards the coast from a signposted turn-off along the Bruce Highway.

VISITOR INFORMATION

The Port Douglas Tourist Information Centre is in 23 Macrossan Street, ✆4099 5599. The relevant website is ☞www.portdouglas.com and there is an email service at ✉reserv@greatbarrierreef.aus.net

ACCOMMODATION AND SERVICES

This place draws visitors like a magnet, but as long as you plan ahead there is little chance of you finding yourself without a bed in Port Douglas. Accommodation abounds, and all budgets are targeted. Here is sample:

Sheraton Mirage Port Douglas, Port Douglas Road, ✆4098 5885. 297 rooms, luxurious facilities, beach frontage, licensed restaurant, golf course, spa, sauna, pool, gym, tennis - ✪$490-670 (3 suites - $1900-2100).

Balboa Apartments, 1 Garrick Street, ✆4099 5222. 10 units, undercover parking, pool, spa - ✪$280-350.

Radisson Reef Resort, Port Douglas Road, ✆4099 5577. 180 units, children's facilities, 2 licensed restaurants, playground, putting green, pool, tennis, gym - ✪$185-280.

Tropical Nites, 119 Davidson Street, ✆4099 9666. 12 units, undercover parking, pool - ✪$95-145.

Port Douglas Tropic Sands, 21 Davidson Street, ℰ4099 4533. 14 units, pool, barbecue, secure parking - ✪$90-125.

Hibiscus Gardens, cnr Owen & Mowbray Streets, ℰ4099 5315. 34 units, undercover parking, barbecue, pool, spa - ✪$80-180.

Pelican Inn, 123 Davidson Street, ℰ4099 5266. 17 units, licensed restaurant (closed Sun), undercover parking, pool - ✪$89-99.

Coconut Grove, 58 Macrossan Street, ℰ4099 5124. 22 units, undercover parking, licensed restaurant, pool - ✪$55-75.

Caravan Parks

Glengarry Caravan Park, Mowbray River Road, ℰ4098 5922. 80 sites, barbecue, playground, pool - powered sites ✪$18 for two, cabins $60 for two.

Pandanus Van Park, 97-107 Davidson Street, ℰ4099 5944. 100 sites, pool, barbecue - powered sites ✪$17, cabins $50-65.

Eating Out

For Chinese dining, you can visit **Han Court**, 85 Davidson Street, ℰ4099 5007, or **Jade Inn**, 35 Macrossan Street, ℰ4099 5974. **Chief's**, 43 Macrossan Street, ℰ4099 4199, serves Mexican, while **Sardi's**, 123 Davidson Street, ℰ4099 5266, serves Italian cuisine and also has a bar.

Three other restaurants you may like to try are **Taste of Thailand**, 12 Macrossan Street, ℰ4399 4384, **Whispers**, 20 Langley Road, ℰ4099 3877 and **Nautilus**, 17 Murphy Street, ℰ4099 5330.

POINTS OF INTEREST

Flagstaff Hill offers a great view over Four Mile Beach.

The **Rainforest Habitat** in Port Douglas Road, ℰ4099 3235, has over 300m of elevated walkways with thousands of butterflies, native birds, crocodiles, koalas and wallabies set among waterways and shaded tropical gardens. They have over 1,000 animals representing more than 140 species. *Breakfast With the Birds* and *The Koala Spot* are two popular attractions. The Habitat is ⊙open daily from 8am-5.30pm, with admission prices at ✪$16 adults and $6 children.

Cairns

Ben Cropp's Shipwreck Treasure Trove Museum, is located on Ben Cropp's Wharf, ✆4099 5488, and houses nautical exhibits of historical significance, including Spanish galleons, a century-and-a-half-old wreck and a lost loot. It is ⏰open daily 9am-5pm and admission is ✪$5 adults, $2 children.

The Bally Hooley Steam Express travels through Mossman and its countryside to the sugar mill. For more details, contact the Information Centre in Grant Street, ✆4099 5051.

Tours and Cruises

Quicksilver Cruises offer voyages to Agincourt Reef on the Outer Barrier Reef, and to the Low Isles. Trips are made on a high-speed Wavepiercer Catamaran for the Outer Reef, on a Reef Platform for slow cruising and coral viewing, and on the 30m Wavedancer for sailing around the coral cays. Cruises depart Marina Mirage at 10am daily. Outer Reef Cruises start from ✪$135 and include lunch, morning and afternoon tea, commentary, snorkelling equipment and coral viewing. Trips on the Wavedancer start from ✪$92. For information and bookings, ✆4099 4455.

Quicksilver Connections also have day trip coach tours, including skyrail and cultural tours from ✪$30-75, ✆4099 4455.

Helicopter flights with *Heli-Adventures* are available over reef and rainforest, and to golf courses and rafting expeditions, ✆4034 9066.

A number of other tours may be taken from the town, including horsetrail riding (*Mowbray Valley Trails*, ✆4099 3268) a regular catamaran service to Cooktown, rainforest hiking, 4WD safaris (*Australian Rainforest Safari*, ✆4094 1388), coach trips and reef tours (*Synergy Reef Sailing*, ✆4099 4696).

COOKTOWN to CAIRNS

MAP B

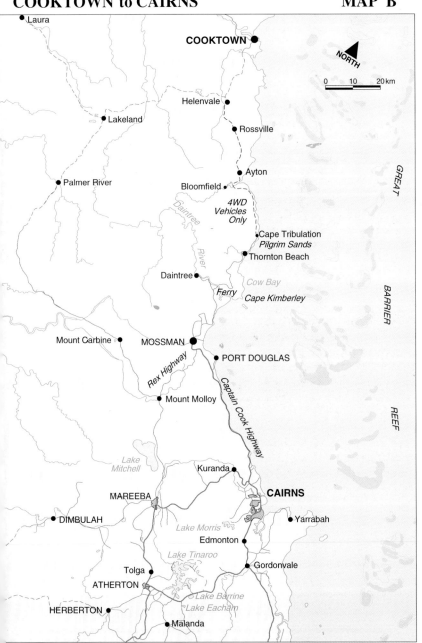

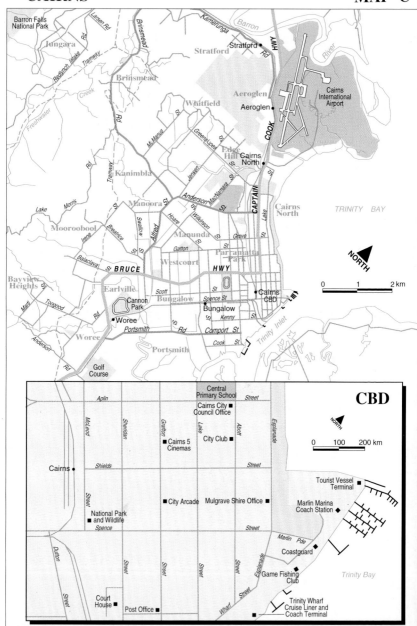

CAIRNS

MAP C

Barron Falls
National Park

Jungara

Brinsmead

Redlynch Intake

Larsen Rd

Tramway

Freshwater Creek

Whitfield

McManus St

Greenslopes St

Kamerunga

Barron River

Stratford

Stratford

COOK HWY

Aeroglen

Cairns
International
Airport

Aeroglen

Edge
Hill

Cairns
North

Kamilbla

Tamburine Rd

Jensen St

McNamara St

Anderson St

CAPTAIN COOK HWY

Lake St

Cairns
North

TRINITY BAY

Lake Morris Rd

Mooroobool

Irene St

Breatrice St

Swallow St

Alfred St

Manoora St

Wilkenson St

Hoare St

Manunda

Grove St

Gatton St

Westcourt

Parramatta
Park

NORTH

0   1   2 km

Bayview
Heights

Marti St

Toogood Rd

Balaclava St

BRUCE HWY

Earlville

Scott St

Bungalow

Cannon
Park

Spence St

Cairns
CBD

LILY

Woree

Portsmith Rd

Bungalow

Kenny St

Anderson Rd

Woree

Comport St

Cook St

Trinity Inlet

Portsmith

Golf
Course

CBD

Aplin

Central
Primary School Street

McLeod Street

Sheridan Street

Grafton Street

Lake Street

Abbott Street

Esplanade

Cairns City
Council Office

City Club

Cairns 5
Cinemas

NORTH

0   100   200 km

Shields Street

Street

Cairns

Tourist Vessel
Terminal

City Arcade

Mulgrave Shire Office

Marlin Marina
Coach Station

National Park
and Wildlife

Spence Street

Street

Marlin Pde

Coastguard

Dutton Street

Street

Street

Street

Street

Esplanade

Game Fishing
Club

Trinity Bay

Court
House

Post Office

Wharf Street

Trinity Wharf
Cruise Liner and
Coach Terminal

GREEN ISLAND

Map J

LOCATION AND CHARACTERISTICS

The island has an area of 15ha and is 27km north-east of Cairns. It is a true coral cay surrounded by coral reefs, and has the only 5-star resort on a coral cay in Great Barrier Reef Marine Park. Incidentally, this island was also named by Captain Cook, after his chief astronomer.

The island grew out of debris washed from its surrounding platform of coral, and is gradually being pushed north-west by prevailing currents. The waters abound with sea life, and the beach is quite beautiful. It only takes about 20 minutes to walk around the island, passing tropical vegetation, fringing casuarinas and pandanus.

Green Island's Underwater Observatory is well known. From 5m below the surface, the ever-changing panorama of marine life can be seen through portholes. Marineland Melanesia has been the island's main attraction for many years.

Green Island is very popular with day trippers.

HOW TO GET THERE

By Sea

Great Adventures Outer Reef and Island Cruises, Wharf Street, Cairns, has a fast, daily catamaran service that departs from Cairns at 8.30am, 10.30am, 1pm, 3.30pm and 9.30pm (Tue, Wed & Fri). Fares are ✪$44 adults and $22 children. You can also visit the island as part of a cruise to Fitzroy Island and the Outer Barrier Reef. For enquiries, ✆1800 079 080 and to book, ✆4051 0455. Note that transfers are included in the tariff if you are staying at the resort.

VISITOR INFORMATION

For information on Green Island, either contact the Green Island Resort directly, ✆4031 3300, visit the web page at:

👁www.greenislandresort.com.au

Or email them at ✉res@greenislandresort.com.au

ACCOMMODATION AND SERVICES

The *Green Island Resort* has deluxe guest rooms and reef suites.

Resort facilities are: restaurants, pool bar, two swimming pools, resort shops, dive centre, sailboards, snorkelling, surf skis, canoes, nature activities and a guest reception lounge in Cairns.

Unit facilities are: private bathroom with shower and bath, tea/coffee making facilities, air conditioning, ceiling fans, mini bar, refrigerator, colour TV, in-house movies, IDD/STD telephone, balcony, in-room safe and bath robes.

Tariffs for a double room per night are:

Island Suite - ✪$440

Reef Suite - ✪$550

The above rates are room only and include free use of beach hire equipment, guest library, underwater observatory, snorkelling equipment, fish feeding and activities, and transfers ex Cairns.

POINTS OF INTEREST

Apart from the facilities and activities listed above, the island also has its own resident attraction. **Marineland Melanesia**, ✆4051 4032, is an underwater observatory which also features Cassius, the largest salt water crocodile in captivity. It has interesting displays of Melanesian tribal art, and a collection of early Coral Sea sailing relics. Interest in the observatory draws many people out to Green Island for the day. There are shows at 10.30am and 1.45pm, daily. Marineland Melanesia is ⏱open 9.30am-4.30pm every day and costs adults ✪$7 and children $3.

MARLIN COAST - NORTHERN BEACHES

Map J

LOCATION AND CHARACTERISTICS

The Marlin Coast area extends from Machans Beach, at the mouth of the Barron River 13km (8 miles) north of Cairns to Ellis Beach, passing by Holloways Beach, Yorkeys Knob, Clifton Beach, Palm Cove and Kewarra Beach.

Cairns

Trinity Beach and Clifton Beach are popular holiday destinations, and Palm Cove and Kewarra Beach have international resorts.

HOW TO GET THERE

By Bus

There are regular bus services from Cairns. The charter company, Marlin Sunbus, operates from the City Centre Bus Terminal in Cairns, ✆4057 7411.

By Car

The southern Marlin Coast settlements can be reached by turning east off the Captain Cook Highway at signposted points. The townships of Clifton Beach, Palm Cove and Ellis Beach lie on or near the highway, further north.

VISITOR INFORMATION

Trinity Beach and Yorkeys Knob have their own web sites:

👁www.trinitybeach.com and email at ✎info@trinitybeach.com

👁www.yorkeysknob.com and email at ✎hmbr@internetnorth.com.au

For other information on the Marlin Coast, use the same contact details as those listed under Tourist Information for *Cairns*.

ACCOMMODATION AND SERVICES

There is plenty of accommodation along the entire stretch of the Marlin Coast settlements. Below is an overview of what is on offer.

Yorkeys Knob

Cairns Golden Sands Boutique Resort, 12-14 Deauville Close, ✆4055 8033. 30 units, licensed restaurant, undercover parking, tennis court, pool - ✪$120-147.

Half Moon Bay Resort, 101 Wattle Street, ✆4055 8059 or ✆1800 810 010 (toll free). 19 units, undercover parking, pool, spa - ✪$95-115.

Villa Marine, 8 Rutherford Street, ✆4055 7322. 9 units, barbecue, pool - ✪$70.

Cairns Yorkeys Knob Beachfront Van Park, 73 Sims Esplanade, ✆4055 7201. 32 sites, barbecue - powered sites ✪$18 for two.

Eating Out

If you wish to eat out, there is the **Blue Horizons Restaurant** at the Golden Sands Boutique Resort, 12-14 Deauville Close, ℰ4055 8633; **La Provencal**, Deauville Close, ℰ4055 8028; or **Chinese & Thai Takeaway**, 455 Varley Street, ℰ4081 0100.

Kewarra Beach

Kewarra Beach Resort, off Captain Cook Highway, ℰ4057 6666. 76 units (four varieties), licensed restaurant, tennis court, swimming pool - ✪$97-195.

Trinity Beach

Coral Sands Resort, cnr Trinity Beach Road & Vasey Esplanade, ℰ4057 8800. Licensed restaurant, security parking, pool - ✪$146-280.

Marlin Gateway Apartments, 33 Trinity Street, ℰ4057 7600. 16 units, undercover parking, pool - ✪$105-125.

Tranquil Trinity, 154 Trinity Beach Road, ℰ4057 5759. 3 rooms, parking, pool, spa - ✪$65-75.

Tropic Sun Holiday Units, 46 Moore Street, ℰ4055 6619 or ℰ1800 805 708 (toll free). 4 units, parking, pool - ✪$55-75.

Wintersun Caravan Park, 116 Trinity Beach Road, ℰ4055 6306. 68 sites, pool - powered sites ✪$16 for two.

Eating Out

Restaurants in the area include, **Avanti BYO Trattoria**, 47 Vasey Esplanade, ℰ4057 7515; **Blue Waters at the Beach**, 77 Vasey Esplanade, ℰ4055 6194; and **Chalet Swiss**, Shop 9, Coastwatcher Centre, ℰ4055 6122.

Clifton Beach

Agincourt Beachfront Apartments, 69 Arlington Esplanade, ℰ4055 3500. 45 units, undercover parking, transfers, pool - ✪$115-135.

Kaikea, 16 Eddy Street, ℰ4059 0010. 2 rooms, spa, pool - bed & breakfast ✪$70.

Clifton Sands, cnr Guide Street & Clifton Road, ✆4055 3355. 18 units, undercover parking, pool - ✪$65-75.

Paradise Gardens Caravan Resort, cnr Clifton Road & Captain Cook Highway, ✆4055 3712. 80 sites, barbecue, playground, pool - powered sites ✪$17.50 for two.

Billabong Caravan Park, Captain Cook Highway, ✆4055 3737. 40 sites, barbecue, playground, pool - powered sites ✪$17, units $45-59.

Eating Out

You can dine out at ***Clifton Capers Bar & Grill***, 14 Clifton Road, ✆4059 2311; or ***Serenata Pizza & Pasta***, Captain Cook Highway, ✆4055 3699.

Palm Cove

Villa Paradiso, 111 Williams Esplanade, ✆4055 3300. 19 units, cooking facilities, secure parking, spa, pool - ✪$250-340.

Novotel Palm Cove Resort, Coral Coast Drive, ✆4059 1234. 343 rooms, 72 suites, licensed restaurant, playground, transfers, golf course, gym, squash, tennis courts, sauna, pool, spa, sailing, windsurfing - ✪$195-400.

The Allamanda Palm Cove, 1 Veivers Road, ✆4055 3000. 70 units, licensed restaurant, secure parking, pool, spa - ✪$195-460.

Coconut Lodge, 95 Williams Esplanade, ✆4055 3734. 16 units, barbecue, playground, secure parking - ✪$59-95.

Melalaeuca Resort, 85 Williams Esplanade, ✆4055 3222. 21 units, barbecue, undercover parking, transfers, pool, spa - ✪$125-150.

Silvester Palms, 32 Veivers Road, ✆4055 3831. 7 units, barbecue, pool - ✪$80-90.

Eating Out

Palm Cove has several restaurants, such as ***Clippers***, 73 Williams Esplanade, ✆4059 0013; ***Far Horizons***, 1 Veivers Road, ✆4055 3000; ***Pisces Live Seafood Restaurant***, Paradise Village Shopping Centre, Williams Esplanade, ✆4055 3200; and ***The Coach House***, Captain Cook Highway, ✆4055 3544.

Cairns

Ellis Beach

Ellis Beach Oceanfront Bungalows & Leisure Park, Captain Cook Highway, ✆4055 3538. 61 sites, barbecue, pool - powered sites ✪$17 for two, units $60 for two, cabins $49 for two.

POINTS OF INTEREST

Two attractions are located on the magnificent Cook Highway, both of which are popular with tourists and locals alike.

40km north of Cairns is **Hartley's Creek Crocodile Farm**, ✆4055 3576, where admission rates are ✪$14.50 for adults, $7 children and $36 for a family pass. **Wild World**, ✆4055 3669 at Palm Cove along the same stretch of road 20 minutes north of Cairns, is a wildlife sanctuary with a hands-on approach. It is ⏰open daily 8.30am-5pm and costs ✪$20 for adults and $10 for children, with family passes available.

All beaches have picnic areas and regular bus services to and from Cairns. Palm Cove and Ellis Beach are regularly patrolled in the summer season by the local Life Saving Club members. Watersporters can hire catamarans, windsurfers and surf skis at most of the major beaches in the area. Countless cruises to the coral creefs are also available, and the Visitor Information Centre can advise.

Yorkeys Knob has the popular **Half Moon Bay Golf Course**, ✆4055 8059, a pleasant 18-hole, par 67 course that costs ✪$20 for a full round, $25 to hire a cart, and $10 for clubs.

The Novotel Resort at Palm Cove also has a **Golf Course**. Here it costs ✪$25 for 18 holes, $15 to hire clubs and $25 for a motorised cart, ✆4059 1234.

CAIRNS

Map C
Population 130,000

The Far North Queensland region extends from Cardwell in the south to the Torres Strait in the north, and west across the Gulf of Carpentaria to the Northern Territory border, an area of 377,796 sq km

(145,829 sq miles) which is almost twice the size of the state of Victoria. Cairns, its major city and service, administration, distribution and manufacturing centre, has recorded the second highest percentage of population growth of any Australian city since 1979. In fact, it was named Australia's most livable regional centre back in 1995.

CLIMATE

Average temperature: January max 32C (90F) - min 24C (75F); July max 25C (77F) - min 16C (61F). The humidity is high in summer, and the best time to visit is from May to October.

CHARACTERISTICS

Cairns, in the heart of the tropical wonderland, is an international tourist mecca. It is a modern, colourful city situated on the shores of a natural harbour, Trinity Inlet, with a magnificent backdrop of rugged mountains covered with thick tropical rainforest.

The major glamour activity in Cairns is Big Game Fishing, and numerous fish over 450kg (992 lb) are caught each year. The game fishing season starts in early September and continues through to late November, however light game can be caught all year round.

As well as being a major city for tourism, Cairns is an important centre for the export of sugar and the agricultural products of the Atherton Tablelands.

The city was named after William Wellington Cairns, the third Governor of Queensland.

HOW TO GET THERE

By Air

Ansett, ℂ13 1300, and Qantas, ℂ13 1313 have frequent daily flights to Cairns from major southern ports.

Sunstate Airlines, ℂ13 1313, operate daily flights to/from Cairns, Cooktown and Thursday Island, along with scheduled services to other centres.

Cairns

Flight West, ℐ1300 130 092, is another option when travelling internally around northern Queensland.

Cairns International Airport accepts many international airlines including Qantas, Thai International, Air Nuigini, Continental, Air New Zealand and Japan Airlines.

Cairns' Domestic and International airports, ℐ4052 9703, are approximately 6km from the centre of the city. Regular coach services depart from the domestic terminals for the city and the northern beaches, and there is also an inter-terminal coach service.

By Rail

The Queenslander and The Sunlander operate regular services from Brisbane to Cairns. Both services provide sleeping berths, sitting cars, dining and club cars, and a lounge car. Single economy fares for The Queenslander are ✪$142 adults and $71 concession, and passengers have the option of taking their private vehicles on this service. Single economy fares for The Sunlander are ✪$177 adults and $106 concession. The Brisbane to Cairns trip takes about 32 hours on these fast and luxurious trains. For more information, ℐ132 235.

By Bus

Greyhound Pioneer, ℐ13 2030, and McCafferty's, ℐ13 1499, operate regular daily express coach services from major southern cities.

By Road

From Brisbane, via the Bruce Highway, it is a four day trip covering 1,720km (1,070 miles).

From the north, access is via the Captain Cook Highway.

VISITOR INFORMATION

The Visitors Information Centre is on the Cairns Esplanade (near the pier complex). ☉Open 7 days, 9.30am-5.30pm.

For information relating to all areas in North Queensland, contact Tourism Tropical North Queensland on ℐ 4051 3588 or at:

✉ ttnq@tnq.org.au

If you wish, visit the website at ☞www.tnq.org.au

The Great Barrier Reef Visitors Bureau has developed a web site encompassing the entire region, with detailed and up-to-date information on accommodation, sightseeing, tours and more for every major locality. The address is:
👁www.greatbarrierreef.aus.net
with email at ✒visitors@greatbarrierreef.aus.net

ACCOMMODATION

The Cairns area has over 40 motels, as well as hotels, guest houses, holiday apartments and over 20 caravan parks. Prices vary considerably depending on the standard of accommodation and the season. Here we have a selection, with prices for a double room per night, which should be used as a guide only. The telephone area code is 07.

Radisson Plaza Hotel, Marlin Parade, ✆4031 1411. 219 rooms, 22 suites, licensed restaurants, swimming pool, spa, sauna, gym - ✪$275-320.

Cairns Hilton Hotel, Wharf Street, ✆4050 2000 or ✆1800 222 255 (toll free). 260 rooms, 5 suites, licensed restaurant, 3 cocktail bars, coffee shop, barbecue area, swimming pool, fitness centre, spa, sauna, beauty salon, shopping, tour desk, garage parking - ✪$250.

Holiday Inn Cairns, cnr Esplanade & Florence Street, ✆5050 6070. 232 rooms, 6 suites, licensed restaurant, bars, swimming pool - ✪$240-265.

Cairns International Hotel, 17 Abbot Street, ✆4031 1300 or ✆1800 079 100 (toll free). 339 rooms, 18 suites, licensed restaurant (closed Sunday), cocktail bars, coffee shop, entertainment, barbecue area, swimming pool, fitness centre, spa, 2 saunas, beauty salon, shopping, tour desk - ✪$180-270.

Righa Colonial Club Resort, 18 Cannon Street, Manunda, ✆4053 5111. 79 units, licensed restaurants, 3 swimming pools, tennis court, courtesy coach transfers and shuttle to and from the city - ✪$175.

Cairns

Bay Village Tropical Retreat, 227 Lake Street, ✆4051 4622. 63 rooms, licensed restaurant, room service, bar, swimming pool, courtesy coach to airport - ✪$112-175.

Hides Hotel, cnr Lake & Shields Streets, ✆4051 1266. 70 rooms with private facilities, some with shared facilities, swimming pool, spa, bistro, bars, 24 hour security - ✪$110.

Ocean Blue Resort Cairns, 702 Bruce Highway, ✆4054 4444. 36 units, licensed restaurant, bar, swimming pool - ✪$105

Country Comfort Outrigger, cnr Abbott & Florence Streets, ✆4051 6188. 90 units, licensed restaurant, bar, coffee shop, swimming pool, spa - ✪$99-129.

Acacia Court, 223 The Esplanade, ✆4051 5011. 145 hotel style rooms, 16 motel units, licensed restaurant, lounge, bar, swimming pool - ✪$99-110.

Flying Horseshoe, 281 Sheridan Street, ✆4051 3022. 51 units, licensed restaurant, swimming pool, spa, games room - ✪$89-99.

Cairns Holiday Lodge, 259 Sheridan Street, cnr Thomas Street, ✆4051 4611. 35 units, licensed restaurant, swimming pool, courtesy bus - ✪$85-90.

G'Day Tropical Village Resort, 7 McLachlan Street, Manunda, ✆4053 7555. 68 studio units, licensed restaurant, swimming pool - ✪$80-95.

Great Northern, 69 Abbott Street, ✆4051 5966. 33 rooms - ✪$79.

Cairns Tropical Gardens, 312 Mulgrave Road, ✆4031 2605. 55 units, licensed restaurant open Mon-Sat, pool, spa, sauna - ✪$75-80.

A1 Motel, 211 Sheridan Street, ✆4051 4499. 31 units, 1 suite, licensed restaurant and bar, swimming pool - ✪$60-62.

Adobe, 191 Sheridan Street, ✆4051 5511. 15 units, licensed restaurant, room service, swimming pool - ✪$55-75.

Leo's Budget Accommodation, 100 Sheridan Street, ✆4051 1264. 54 rooms, pool - ✪$30-75.

Caravan Parks

Cairns Coconut Caravan Resort, cnr Bruce Highway & Anderson Road, ✆4054 6644. (No pets) 279 sites, recreation room, barbecue, playground, cafe, transfers, tennis, pool, mini golf, basketball - powered sites ✪$22 for two, cabins $45-59 for two, units $75 for two.

First City Caravilla Caravan Park, Little Street, ✆4054 1403. (No pets) 100 sites, barbecue, playground, kiosk, mini golf, pool - powered sites ✪$18-20 for two, cabins $51-65 for two.

Coles Villa & Leisure Park, 28 Pease Street, Manoora, ✆4053 7133. (No pets) 163 sites, recreation room, lounge, barbecue, playground, shop, pool - powered sites ✪$16-18 for two, units $50-70 for two, cabins $55-75 for two.

Crystal Cascades Holiday Park, Intake Road, Redlynch, ✆4039 1036. 92 sites, recreation room, barbecue area, salt water pool, spa - powered sites ✪$19 for two; villas $50-70 for two.

There are two **Youth Hostels** in the area: *Cairns Esplanade*, 93 The Esplanade, ✆4031 1919. 18 rooms, ✪$20 per person twin share; and *Cairns-McLeod Street*, 20-24 McCleod Street, ✆4051 0772. 30 rooms - ✪$19 per person twin share.

LOCAL TRANSPORT

There are public transport services to all Cairns city areas, suburbs and beaches. Timetables and routes are available at hotels and bus depots.

Cairns City Airporter, ✆4031 3555, have an airport/city/airport service, and bookings are essential for trips to the airport. They also have vehicles available for charter.

Coral Coaches, ✆4031 7577, have daily services between: Cairns, Hartley Creek, Port Douglas, Mossman, Daintree, Cape Tribulation, Bloomfield, Cooktown - Inland and Coast Road. They also have airport transfers to/from: Northern Beaches, Port Douglas, Mossman and Cape Tribulation.

Whitecar Coaches, ✆4051 9533, service the Atherton Tablelands and Chillagoe.

Cairns

CAR HIRE

Avis, 135 Lake Street, ℭ4051 5911, and Cairns International Airport, ℭ4035 9100.

All Car Rentals, 30 Grafton Street, ℭ4031 6322.

Cairns Tropical Rent-A-Car, 141 Lake Street, Cairns, ℭ4031 3995.

Hertz, 436 Sheridan Street, Cairns, ℭ4053 6701.

Mini Car Rentals, 150 Sheridan Street, Cairns, ℭ4051 6288.

Peter's Economy Rent-A-Car, 36 Water Street, Cairns, ℭ4051 4106.

Cairns Leisure Wheels, 314 Sheridan Street, Cairns, ℭ4051 8988.

National Car Rental, 135 Abbott Street, Cairns, ℭ1800 350 536.

Honeycombs Cars & 4WD's, 303-307 Mulgrave Road, Cairns, ℭ4051 9211.

ENTERTAINMENT

Cairns has nightclubs, discos, karaoke bars, theatre restaurants, live theatre and cinemas. There are street musicians and all types of performing artists in and around the shopping areas, taverns and bars.

Club International & My Karaoke Bar, 40 Lake Street, ℭ4052 1480.

Sports Bar, 33 Spence Street, ℭ4041 2533.

The Beach Nite Club, 78 Abbott Street, ℭ4031 3944.

The Cat House Night Club, 78 Abbott Street, ℭ4051 6322.

Because the weather is quite warm at night there are always lots of people to be found along the Esplanade, eating at pavement tables, or picnicking on the lawns.

Cairns also has a couple of clubs who welcome visitors and offer free temporary membership for those who live more than 40km from the club.

Brothers Leagues Club (Cairns), 99 Anderson Street, Manunda, ℭ4053 1053.

The Yacht Club, 4 The Esplanade (between Hilton Hotel and Great Adventures), ℭ4031 2750.

SHOPPING

There are plenty of shopping opportunities in Cairns. The large hotels have boutiques offering imported fashion items and jewellery, and then there is *The Pier Marketplace*, ℭ4051 7244, in Pierpoint Road. The Pier is a landmark in Cairns. The building contains the Radisson Plaza Hotel and a specialty retail leisure centre.

It has separate theme walkways, the most glamorous of which is the Governor's Way, where Cairns' best fashion stores and boutiques are found. The main entrance leads to Trader's Row, which has a colonial air and some appealing shops that are not the usual 'high fashion'.

The *Mud Markets* are held on Saturday and Sunday in the main amphitheatre of the specialty retail centre, and local artisans and artists set up stalls selling all sorts of interesting objects from handcrafts to glassware. Live entertainers roam around the markets, creating a really festive atmosphere.

The Pier Marketplace is ◷open daily 9am-9pm, but most of the shops in the city centre are open Mon-Thurs 8.30am-8pm, Fri 8.30am-9pm, Sat 8.30am-5.30pm, Sun 3-8pm. Those in the suburbs have shorter hours with night shopping on one night only.

EATING OUT

Cairns has some of the best eating places in Queensland. Most of the international standard hotels and motels have at least one restaurant as well as a bistro, or the like. There is also a good selection of restaurants, some of which can be found along the Cairns Esplanade, where you can enjoy both the meal and views of the natural harbour inlet. Here is a selection of restaurants in the area:

Tawny's Seafood Restaurant, Marlin Parade, ✆4051 1722. Seafood specialists with an a-la-carte menu. Open 5.30pm-midnight 7 days, closed on Public Holidays.

Golden Sun Inn, 313 Kamerunga Road, Freshwater, ✆4055 1177. Chinese cuisine, BYO and licensed. Open 5pm-10pm every day except Tuesday and Public Holidays.

Tandoori Oven, 62 Shields Street, ✆4031 0043. Open 6.30pm-10.30pm daily, closed Sunday and Public Holidays.

Thai Pan Restaurant, 43-45 Grafton Street, ✆4052 1708. Licensed and BYO, take-away and free home delivery available. Open 6pm-8pm every day.

Cosmo On The Bay, The Esplanade Centre, ✆4031 5400. Cosmopolitan dining, seafood is a speciality. Open 5.30pm-11.30pm daily, and for lunch and extended hour on Thursdays, Fridays and Sundays.

Jango Jango Club Restaurant, Level 1 Palm Court, 34 Lake Street, ©4031 2411. Asian influenced fare and karaoke. Open 6pm-2am daily.

Brothers Leagues Club (Cairns), 99 Anderson Street Cairns, ©4053 1053. Betting and gambling facilities. Open 9am-11pm daily except on Public Holidays.

The Sorrento, 70 Grafton Street, ©4051 7841. Italian cuisine, pizza, seafood and steak.

Red Ochre Grill, 43 Shields St, ©4051 0100. Modern Australian cuisine with seafood and outdoor dining facilities. Open 10am-11pm Mon-Sat, 3pm-11pm Sunday and Public Holidays.

Aphrodisias Restaurant, 82 Sheridan Street, ©4051 5871.

McDonalds is in both the Cairns Central Shopping Centre and on the Esplanade. KFC is at Shop 5, 71-75 The Esplanade and at the corner of Mulgrave and Florence Streets. Pizza Hut is on the corner of Aurnullar Street & Mulgrave Road, ©13 1166.

POINTS OF INTEREST

There are no sandy beaches in Cairns itself, only mudflats, but prolific birdlife gathers here. Palms line many streets, with parks and gardens displaying a riot of colour from bougainvillaea, hibiscus, poinciana and other tropical blooms. The old part of town is to be found around Wharf Street and The Esplanade. The National Trust has put out a walking tour brochure about this part of town.

The Esplanade is 5km (3 miles) long and runs along the side of the bay. This park-like area is a very pleasant place to relax in the cooler part of the day.

The Flecker Botanic Gardens, Collins Avenue, Edge Hill, are ©open daily and feature graded walking tracks through natural rainforest to Mount Whitfield. From here there are excellent views of the city and coastline.

The **Centenary Lakes**, Greenslopes Street, Cairns North, are an extension of Flecker Botanic Gardens and were created to mark the city's centenary in 1976. There are two lakes - one fresh water, the other salt. Bird life abounds and barbecue facilities have been provided. Mount Mooroobool (610m - 2000 ft) in the background is the city's highest peak.

The Pier Marketplace hosts live entertainment daily, and is the departure point for most reef cruises and fishing boat charters. Sit on the verandah for a quick snack or a delicious meal from one of the many food outlets, while checking out the magnificent views over Trinity Inlet.

The Royal Flying Doctor Base, 1 Junction Street, Edge Hill, ℰ4053 5687, has fully guided tours, film shows, and displays of the history and present operations of this legendary service. ☺Open seven days.

Sugarworld Waterslides, Mill Road, Edmonton, ℰ4055 5477, is 14km south of Cairns City centre, and has tropical horticulture, a licensed restaurant, tours, rides and waterslides.

The Reef Hotel Casino, 35-41 Wharf Street, ℰ4030 8888, offers what all casinos offer: a glitzy way to part with your money.

The **Cairns Convention Centre**, cnr Wharf & Sheridan Streets, ℰ4042 4200, may have a function on at the time of your visit.

FESTIVALS
The festival season begins with the Mareeba Rodeo in early July and then onto the Cairns Show for three days of entertainment.

The Cairns Amateur Horserace Meeting is held in September, and the week-long Fun in the Sun Festival is in October.

SPORTS
All types of water sports are catered for, as well as the usual sporting activities.

DIVING
The following companies in Cairns offer diving trips and lessons.

Cairns

Pro Dive, 116 Spence Street, ©4031 5255. 5 day learn to dive courses are held 4 times weekly. 3 day/2 night liveaboard cruises 4 times weekly - PADI 5-Star facility.

Deep Sea Divers Den, Wharf Street, ©4031 5622. Dive and snorkel trips, dive courses (beginner to instructor level), diving/fishing charters on the Outer Barrier Reef.

Taka 2 Dive Adventures, 131 Lake Street, ©4051 8722. Offer dives in Cod Hole, Ribbon Reefs, Coral Sea - liveaboard, departs bi-weekly.

Great Diving Adventures Cairns, Wharf Street, ©4051 4444. PADI open water dive courses available on tropical Fitzroy Island, including accommodation, meals, transfers and certification - other great dive locations include Norman Reef and Michaelmas Cay, both on the Outer Barrier Reef.

TOURS

Cairns is a staging place for tours to the Great Barrier Reef, the Islands, the Atherton Tablelands, the Barron Gorge, Cooktown and Cape Tribulation. Here are a few.

The *Cairns Explorer* bus leaves from Lake Street Transit Mall every hour 9am-4pm Mon-Sat. It visits Wescourt shopping, Earlville shopping, Freshwater swimming hole, Freshwater Connection, Mangrove Boardwalk, Botanical Gardens, Flying Doctor and Centenary Lakes. For bookings and enquiries, ©4033 5344.

Wait A-While Environmental Wildlife Tours, 5 Alkoo Close, Bayview Heights, ©4033 1153. Day/night wildlife tours - the best way to see the rainforest, birds and animals of North Queensland - small groups, 4WD, experienced guides - departs 2pm daily and costs adults ✪$120.

Tropic Wings Luxury Coach Tours, 278 Hartley Street, ©4035 3555. Specialise in day tours around Cairns and The Tropical North - Atherton Tablelands, Port Douglas & Daintree, Cape Tribulation, Chillagoe, 3 day Outback and Gulf.

Down Under Tours, Cairns, © 4035 5566. Offer tours to Kuranda, Daintree/Port Douglas, The Tablelands, Cairns and Orchid Valley, Weatherby Station (outback).

CAIRNS to TOWNSVILLE

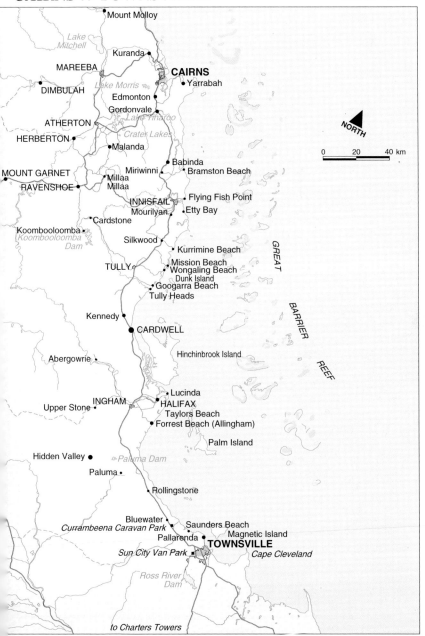

Mount Molloy

Lake Mitchell

Kuranda

MAREEBA

CAIRNS

Yarrabah

DIMBULAH

Lake Morris

Edmonton

Gordonvale

ATHERTON

Lake Tinaroo

HERBERTON

Crater Lakes

Malanda

0   20   40 km

MOUNT GARNET

Miriwinni   Babinda

Bramston Beach

Millaa

RAVENSHOE   Millaa

INNISFAIL   Flying Fish Point

Mourilyan   Etty Bay

Koombooloomba

Cardstone

Koombooloomba Dam

Silkwood

Kurrimine Beach

GREAT

TULLY   Mission Beach

Wongaling Beach

Dunk Island

Googarra Beach

Tully Heads

Kennedy

BARRIER

CARDWELL

Abergowrie   Hinchinbrook Island

REEF

Lucinda

INGHAM   HALIFAX

Upper Stone   Taylors Beach

Forrest Beach (Allingham)

Palm Island

Hidden Valley   Paluma Dam

Paluma

Rollingstone

Bluewater

Currambeena Caravan Park   Saunders Beach

Pallarenda   Magnetic Island

TOWNSVILLE

Sun City Van Park   Cape Cleveland

Ross River Dam

to Charters Towers

TOWNSVILLE

MAP E

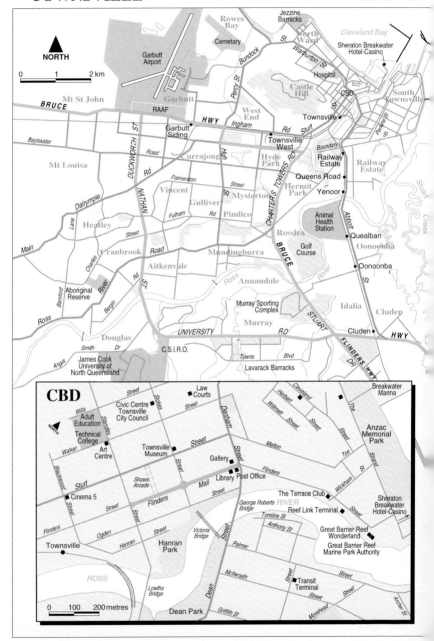

Australian Pacific Tours, 278 Hartley Street, Cairns, ✆4041 9419 or ✆1300 655 965 (reservations). They have an extensive range of half and full days tours, as well as extended tours from 2 to 12 days.

Wilderness Challenge, 15 Tranguna Street, Trinity Beach, ✆4055 6504. 4WD adventure safaris from 1 to 14 days or charters - travel to Cape York, Hinchinbrook, Cooktown, Daintree, Kakadu, Lava Tubes, and more.

Billy Tea Bush Safaris, 94 Upper Richardson Street, Whitfield, ✆4032 0077. 1 day to 14 day safaris available to Cape York, Alice Springs, Ayers Rock, and more.

Oz Tours Safaris, Captain Cook Highway, Smithfield, ✆4055 9535. 7, 9, 10 and 12 day overland/air or 16 day all overland Cape York safaris. Both camping and accommodated options available - also Cairns-Cape York-Thursday Island.

Barrier Reef Cybertours, Shop 9, 7 Shields Street, ✆4041 0666.

Cairns Eco-Tours, 85 Lake Street, ✆4031 0334.

Cairns Harley Tours, ✆0417 45 4962 (mobile).

CRUISES

Sunlover Cruises, cnr Tingara & Aumuller Streets, ✆4050 1333. Luxurious travel aboard Super-Cats to Moore or Arlington Reef - most innovative reef pontoons afloat, underwater theatre and marine touch tanks, free guided snorkelling tours, delicious buffet lunch - free semi-sub (Moore Reef), Supa Viewer (Arlington Reef), and glass bottom boat rides - all levels of diving catered for - optional helicopter and sea plane joyflights (Moore Reef only) - free guided rainforest walk on Fitzroy Island.

Ocean Spirit Cruises, 33 Lake Street, Cairns, ✆4031 2920. Daily departures aboard the *Ocean Spirit I* or *Ocean Spirit II* sailing vessels, to either Michaelmas or Upolu Cay - delicious tropical seafood buffet available.

Big Cat, Pier Marketplace, ✆4051 0444. Has cruises that depart daily from The Pier at 9am and travel to Green Island - snorkelling, glass bottom boat tours, lunch served on board, submersible reef coral viewer, guided snorkel tours - return Cairns 5pm - from ✪$45 adults.

Cairns

Captain Cook Cruises, Trinity Wharf, ✆ 4031 4433. Offer 3, 4 and 7 day Reef Escape cruises every week - cruise to Hinchinbrook and Dunk Islands, or Cooktown and Lizard Island.

Coral Princess Barrier Reef and Island Cruises, Shop 5, 149 Spence Street, ✆4031 1041. Sails between Cairns and Townsville, calling at island resorts and uninhabited islands for beachcombing, swimming and a tropical barbecue.

Clipper Sailaway Cruises, 287 Draper Street, Cairns, ✆4052 8300. Sail on SV *Atlantic Clipper* - a 140' sailing ship catering for 34 passengers - cruises from Cairns to Lizard Island, Great Barrier Reef, Cape York.

Seahorse Sail & Dive, B16 Marlin Marina, ✆ 4041 1919. Snorkelling, diving, lunch included.

Auspray Seafaris, 125 Aumuller Street, ✆4035 3931.

Sport n Game Fishing Charters, 23 Bolton Street, ✆4053 1828.

Barrier Reef Luxury Cruises, Marlin Marina, ✆4051 3555.

Blue Whaler Charters, Marlin Marina, ✆4051 1414.

SCENIC FLIGHTS

Tiger Moth Scenic Flights, Hangar 8, Tom McDonald Drive, Aeroglen, ✆4035 9400 or ✆4055 9814 (after hours).

Reef Hotel Casino, Cairns

CAIRNS TO TOWNSVILLE

FITZROY ISLAND

Map J

LOCATION AND CHARACTERISTICS

Fitzroy has an area of 4 sq km, and is situated 26km south-east of Cairns. It is only 6km from the mainland and was named by Captain Cook after the Duke of Grafton, a politician of the time.

In 1819 Phillip King reported that Welcome Bay, where the resort is, was a good anchorage for passing ships because of its fresh water and supplies of timber.

In 1877 Fitzroy was made a place of quarantine where Chinese immigrants were to stay for 16 days before completing their journey to the Queensland gold fields. At one stage there were 3000 of them in residence, which lead to near-riot conditions. *This* is the reason for the Chinese graves that are to be found at the site, not the Smallpox that the authorities feared.

HOW TO GET THERE

By Sea

Since this is the only method of transport to the island, include fares in the budget for your trip.

Great Adventures, ✆4051 0455 or ✆1800 079 080, has a fast catamaran service that leaves Cairns three times daily and takes 45 minutes to reach the island. Fares are ✪$36 adult return, $18 child return.

VISITOR INFORMATION

Contact the Fitzroy Island Resort on ✆4051 9588 or ✆1800 079 080 (toll free) or visit the website at ☞www.great- barrier-reef.com/fitzroy

ACCOMMODATION AND SERVICES

The *Fitzroy Island Resort* has 8 cabins and 1 bunkhouse.

Townsville

Resort facilities include: licensed restaurant, bar, kiosk, dive shop, laundry/ironing facilities, swimming pool, volleyball, boutique and EFTPOS.

Beach Cabin facilities are: private facilities, colour TV, hairdryer, tea/coffee making facilities, iron/board, refrigerator, ceiling fans, room serviced daily.

Beach Bunkhouse facilities are: shared rooms, shared bathrooms, linen and blankets, shared kitchen facilities and fans.

Tariffs for a double room per night are:

Beach Cabins -   ✪$340
Beach Bunkhouse - ✪$190 (private room)

Reservations can be made directly through the resort, ✆4051 9588 or ✆1800 079 080 (toll free).

Eating Out

The ***Rainforest Restaurant*** at the resort is open to guests, but it is not a cheap night out. There is a mini-market near the beach house bungalows which has a range of supplies for those who want to cook for themselves.

POINTS OF INTEREST

Fitzroy Island is not a great place for swimming as the beaches tend to be corally rather than sandy, although Nudey Beach has some sand. There are a few walking trails - the round trip to the lighthouse; a short rainforest walk to the Secret Garden; and the walk to Nudey Beach.

Canoes and catamarans are available for use, and sailing is popular. There is good diving water right off-shore, and the Reef is not far away. The resort dive shop hires out all gear for snorkelling and diving, runs courses, and provides daily trips to Moore Reef.

THE ATHERTON TABLELANDS

Maps D and J

LOCATION AND CHARACTERISTICS

Inland from Cairns are the fertile Mareeba, Atherton and Evelyn Tablelands, rising in three gigantic steps from the coastal plains. Jungle-fringed volcanic crater lakes, waterfalls and fertile farmlands, coupled with the only temperate climate in the Australian tropics, lure many visitors to the Tablelands each year. Views from the lookouts on the Kuranda, Gillies, Rex and Palmerston Highways are spectacular.

HOW TO GET THERE

By Train

From Cairns, a steam train runs along a very picturesque route to the Kuranda Railway Station, ℰ4032 3964.

By Car

The major settlements are joined by major highways, and the Visitor Information Centre in Cairns will be able to provide you with clear and precise directions for your chosen destinations.

VISITOR INFORMATION

The Tropical Tableland Promotion Bureau has an outlet at the Old Post Office Gallery Information Centre, Herberton Road, Atherton, ℰ4091 4222. They have a terrific website at ☜www.athertontableland.com and can be emailed at ✎info@athertontableland.com

ACCOMMODATION AND SERVICES

Kuranda

Kuranda Rainforest Resort, Kennedy Highway, ℰ4093 7555. 70 units, licensed restaurant, transfers, tennis, gymnasium, pool, spa - ✪$125-179.

Townsville

Kuranda Caravan Park, off Myola Road, ℭ4093 7316. (No cats) 20 sites, barbecue - powered sites ✪$15, cabins $45-55.

Eating Out

Here is a selection of good restaurants in the area: *Billy's Garden Bar & Barbecue*, Coondoo Street, ℭ4093 7203; *Clohesy Country Gardens*, Clohesy River, Kennedy Highway, ℭ4093 7859; and *Frogs*, 11 Coondoo Street, ℭ4093 7405.

Atherton

Lavender Hill Rural Stay, 1 Favier Road, ℭ4095 8384. Bed & breakfast - ✪$80-100.

Atherton, Maunds Road, ℭ4091 1500. 18 units, licensed restaurant (closed Sunday), undercover parking, pool - ✪$60.

Hinterland, 44 Cook Street, ℭ4091 1885. 16 units, undercover parking - ✪$54.

Mountain View Van Park, 152 Robert Street, ℭ4091 4144. 42 sites, barbecue, playground - powered sites ✪$14 for two, units $39-45 for two.

Atherton Woodlands Tourist Park, 141 Herberton Road, ℭ4091 1407. (No dogs allowed) 60 sites, barbecue, playground, pool - powered sites ✪$16 for two, cabins $42-44 for two.

Eating Out

There are a few restaurants to choose from in Atherton, including *Atherton Chinese Restaurant*, 18 Main Street, ℭ4091 2585; the *Chatterbox Bistro*, 48 Main Street, ℭ4091 4388; the *Grill Room*, 77 Main Street, ℭ4091 1139; *Maree's*, 154 Robert Street, ℭ4091 4936; and *Sami's Cafe Theatre Restaurant*, 18 Main Street, ℭ4091 2585.

Malanda

Travellers Rest, Millaa Millaa Road, ℭ4096 6077. 6 units, barbecue, unlicensed restaurant, secure parking - ✪$90.

Fur n Feathers Rainforest Tree House, Hogan Road, Tarzali, ℭ4096 5364. 4 cottages, rainforest walks, wildlife sanctuary, undercover parking - ✪$85-140.

Malanda Lodge, Millaa Millaa Road, ✆4096 5555. 17 units, licensed restaurant (closed Sunday), par 3 golf course, pool, spa - ✪$68.

Malanda Falls Caravan Park, 38 Park Avenue, ✆4096 5314. 70 sites, barbecue, playground - powered sites ✪$14 for two, units $50 for two.

Eating Out

If you wish to eat out, try the *Diggers Den* in the RSL, 8 Catherine Street, ✆4096 5901.

Millaa Millaa

Iskanda Park Farmstay, Nash Road, ✆4097 2401. 1 cottage, standard facilities - ✪$90-100.

Millaa Millaa Caravan Park, Malanda Road, ✆4097 2290. 22 sites, barbecue - powered sites ✪$12 for two, cabins $25-35 for two.

Eating Out

Christies, 19 Main Street, ✆4097 2126; and *Falls Tea House*, Palmerston Highway, ✆4097 2237, are two restaurants among a very limited variety.

Ravenshoe

Millstream Retreat, Kennedy Highway, ✆4097 6785. 2 cottages, undercover parking - ✪$70.

Possum Valley Rainforest Cottages, Evelyn Central, ✆4097 8177. 2 cottages, barbecue, car parking - ✪$75.

Tall Timbers, Kennedy Highway, ✆4097 6325. 4 units, unlicensed restaurant, undercover parking - ✪$50, powered sites in Caravan Park section $12.50.

Club, Grigg Street, ✆4097 6109. 8 units, licensed restaurant, undercover parking, room service - ✪$48.

POINTS OF INTEREST

Kuranda, a tiny mountain hamlet in the rainforest, is the first stop-off stage on the Tableland journey. The town can be reached by train from Cairns (✆4032 3964) and the ride passes waterfalls and stunning views to the coast before ending at picturesque Kuranda Station.

Kuranda has many attractions:

Pamagirri Dancers, Kennedy Highway, ©4093 9033, is an Aboriginal theatre presenting daily shows based on Dreamtime legends.

Australian Butterfly Sanctuary, 8 Rob Veivers Drive, ©4093 7575, is the largest butterfly farm in the world, listed in the Guinness Book of Records.

The **Kuranda Wildlife Noctarium**, 8 Coondoo Street, ©4093 7334, provides a close-up look at the rarely seen nocturnal inhabitants of the rainforests, and guided walks into the jungle.

Kuranda Riverboat and Rainforest Tours, 24 Coondoo Street, ©4093 7476 or ©0412 159 212 (mobile), have tours of the Barron River and surrounding rainforest area.

The town's main street is lined with galleries, shops and restaurants. The terraced *Kuranda Markets*, at 5 Therwine Street, are considered the best in the north, ©4093 8772.

The **Mareeba/Dimbulah** district, approximately 66 km (41 miles) west of Cairns, is the largest tobacco growing area in Australia.

Atherton, with its red volcanic soil, is the central town of the Atherton Tablelands. Maize silos dominate the skyline.

Malanda is situated in the heart of tropical Australia's only viable dairying district. The Malanda milk factory boasts the longest milk run in the world, which extends as far as Darwin in the Northern Territory.

Millaa Millaa is the waterfall capital of the Tablelands, taking in the Millaa Millaa, Zillie and Elinjaa Falls.

The **Millstream Falls**, south of Ravenshoe, when in flood are the widest waterfalls in Australia.

Herberton is the north's historic mining town, and tin is still produced in the area.

Irvinebank situated near Herberton, is steeped in history. Its tin crushing plant has been in operation since 1890, and it has other historic buildings.

Ravenshoe is situated on the western side of the Evelyn Tablelands, and is the gateway to the back country and gemfields of the north.

Townsville

It is a major timber town providing some of Australia's most beautiful woods. Close by you will find Koombooloomba Dam and Tully Falls, with many walking tracks to Eyrie Lookout.

Some of the individual Tableland attractions include Tinaroo Dam, the Crater National Park, the twin crater lakes of Eacham and Barrine, the Curtin Fig Tree and Herberton Tin Fields. Further north of the Evelyn Tablelands is the Chillagoe Caves National Park, which is accessible by road and air charter from Cairns Airport, ©4052 9703.

THE CASSOWARY COAST

The Cassowary Coast incorporates the towns of Cardwell, Tully and Mission Beach, and is the stepping-off point for the great Hinchinbrook Channel, that is renowned for its barramundi, mangrove jack and many other table fish.

Ferries to Hinchinbrook Island National Park leave from Cardwell, and the town also offers estuary and reef fishing trips. You can also organise fully guided or self drive tours through world heritage forests, and scenic attractions such as the beautiful Murray Falls and the wild Blencoe Falls.

Tully is a sugar town that nestles at the foot of the mountain range. Quite close is the Tully River, famous for its whitewater rapids, and there are many operators in town that are ready to take you whitewater rafting.

Mission Beach has a cassowary reserve, great sandy beaches, and a water taxi service to nearby Dunk Island.

MISSION BEACH

Map D
Population 1,500

LOCATION AND CHARACTERISTICS

At Mission Beach, about halfway between Townsville and Cairns, a chain of Mountains runs down to the sea, and surrounds the small

Townsville

coastal settlements. Offshore lie the North and South Barnard, Dunk and Bedarra Islands, and beyond them, the Great Barrier Reef.

Mission Beach is set on a stretch of 14km of coastline that includes Garners Beach, Bingil Bay, Narragon Beach, Clump Point and Wongaling Beach. There is a daily water taxi service from Mission Beach to nearby Dunk Island, and many visitors choose to stay on the mainland and visit the islands, rather than pay resort prices.

The town is named after the Aboriginal Mission that was set up in 1912 at South Mission Beach, but the first settlers were the Cutten brothers who landed to the north at Bingil Bay in 1882 and founded a farming dynasty. They introduced pineapple growing to this part of Queensland and founded tea and coffee plantations. In 1918 the 'cyclone of the century' levelled the settlements and farms in the district.

Nowadays the main industries are banana and sugar-cane growing, and tourism.

CLIMATE

Dry Season: April-October 18C-26C. Wet Season: November-March 20C-35C. Average annual rainfall, about 2500mm.

CHARACTERISTICS

Four villages comprise the Mission Beach area: South Mission Beach, Bingil Bay, Wongaling Beach and Mission Beach. The region's attractions include 14km of pristine beaches, Dunk Island, the offshore Reef, rainforests, and rafting on the Tully River.

HOW TO GET THERE

By Air

You can fly to Cairns then either rent a car or catch the Mission Beach Bus, ©4068 7400, and Coach Company service, which has regular day and night routes to the four villages. From Cairns, Transtate Airlines, ©13 1528, has a service to Dunk Island nearby.

By Coach

All major bus companies provide regular daily services between Townsville and Cairns, calling into the above towns.

Greyhound Pioneer, ✆13 2030, has 2 southerly services to Wongaling Beach daily, and 3 going north.

McCaffertys, ✆13 1499, services Mission Beach twice daily in both directions.

By Rail

The Queenslander, Sunlander and Spirit of the Tropics trains provide luxury services from Brisbane. For more information, ✆13 2235.

By Car

Mission Beach is on a loop road that branches off the Bruce Highway at Tully and rejoins at El Arish.

VISITOR INFORMATION

The Mission Beach Visitor Information Centre, Porter Promenade, ✆4068 7066, can be found 100 metres from the post office. The Centre has a wealth of information on every part of the area. They can be contacted by email at ✉ visitors@znet.net.au

ACCOMMODATION

What follows is only a selection of accommodation available in Mission Beach and adjoining villages. The prices listed below should be used as a guide only. These figures generally represent an overnight stay for two people, and the range from budget to premium rates has been provided where possible.

The telephone area code is 07.

Castaways Beachfront Resort, cnr Pacific Parade & Seaview Street, ✆4068 7444. 37 units, licensed restaurant, undercover parking, pool, spa - motel ✪$130, suite $230.

Beaches, 82 Reid Road, Wongaling Beach, ✆4068 7411. 5 units, undercover parking, pool - ✪$100-150.

Mission Beach Resort, cnr Cassowary Drive & Wongaling Beach Road, ✆4068 8288. 75 units, undercover parking, pool - ✪$100.

Townsville

Collingwood House, 13 Spurwood Close, Wongaling Beach, ©4068 9037. 3 rooms, barbecue, pool - ✪$85-95

Bingil Bay Resort, The Esplanade, Bigil Bay, ©4068 7208. 16 units, licensed restaurant, pool - ✪$60-80.

Liana Place, cnr Boyett Road and Porter Promenade, ©4068 7411. 4 units, barbecue, playground, undercover parking, pool - ✪$50-90.

Watersedge Beach Apartments, 32 Reid Road, ©4068 8479. 6 units, undercover parking, spa, pool - ✪$45-65.

Caravan Parks

Mission Beach Hideaway Holiday Village, 58-60 Porters Promenade, ©4068 7104. 130 sites, playground, barbecue, pool - powered sites ✪$17-19 for two, cabins $39-59 for two.

Dunk Island View Caravan Park, 175 Reid Road, ©4068 8248. 75 sites, pool, playground, barbecue - powered sites ✪$15 for two, units $47 for two.

There is a **Youth Hostel** in Bingil Bay Road, ©4068 7137, which has 12 rooms at ✪$21 per person twin share.

LOCAL TRANSPORT

Coaches

Coral Coaches, ©4098 2600. Door to door shuttle service, routes from Cairns to Mission Beach, connects with boats to Dunk Island, bookings essential.

Mission Beach Bus Co, ©4068 7400. Operates day and night, 7 days, service from Bingil Bay to South Mission, daily ticket ✪$7.

Water Taxi

Dunk Island Express, ©4068 8310. Mission Beach to Dunk Island return, adult ✪$24, child $12, departs 6 times a day from Wongaling Beach.

Car Rentals

Sugarland Car Rentals, ©4068 8272.

Taxi

Mission Beach Taxis, ©4068 8155, run regularly 24hrs.

EATING OUT

Here are some of the restaurants you will find in Mission Beach:

Friends Restaurant, Beachtown Porter Promenade, ✆4068 7107.

The Horizon at Mission Beach, Explorer Drive, ✆4068 8154.

The Shrubbery Taverna, 44 Marine Parade, ✆4068 7803.

Port O'Call Cafe, Shop 6 Porter Promenade, ✆4068 7390.

Piccolo Paradiso, David Street, Mission Beach, ✆4068 7008.

Wheats Steakhouse, The Village Green, Mission Beach, ✆4068 7850.

Cafe Coconuts, Porter Promenade, Mission Beach, ✆4068 7397.

Blarney's By The Beach, Wongalong Beach Road, Wongalong, ✆4068 8472.

SHOPPING

Markets are a popular form of trade in the Mission Beach area. *Monster Markets* are ☺open every last Sunday of the month from April to November, and *Mission Beach Markets* are held on Porter Promenade opposite Hideaway Caravan Park ☺every first Saturday and third Sunday.

POINTS OF INTEREST

The main activities in Mission Beach involve water sports and reef viewing, so if you wish to view land-based attractions, you will have to travel a little further afield. Here are a few suggestions, and the Visitor Centre can provide you with detailed directions to each.

The **Australian Insect Farm**, Davis Road, Gurradunga, ✆4063 3860, offers regular tours daily Tues-Sun, adults ✪$8, children $6.50.

Paronella Park, Japoonvale Road, Mena Creek, ✆4065 3225, comprises historic rainforest gardens. It is ☺open 9am-5pm and costs adults ✪$10, pensioners $8 and children $5.

The Australian Sugar Industry Museum, Bruce Highway, Mourilyan, ✆4063 2656, has a wealth of memorabilia from old harvesters to historical photographs.

Johnstone River Crocodile Farm, Flying Fish Point Road, Innisfail, ✆4061 1121, facilitates crocodile breeding and displays wildlife. It is ☺open 7 days 8.30am-4.30pm, adults ✪$11, children $5, family pass $28.

Townsville

In addition, trips can be taken to these popular environmental destinations: Tully Gorge, Hinchinbrook Island, Murray Falls and the Atherton Tablelands.

FESTIVALS

The premier event in Mission Beach is the Aquatic Festival, held in October, ✆4068 7066. Fishing and sailing competitions are organised regularly throughout the year.

SPORTS

Bush'n'Beach Horse Rides, ✆4068 7893. 1 and a half hours ✪$38; half day (refreshments provided) $69.

Coral Sea Kayaking, Dunk Island, ✆4068 9154. Including snorkelling and lunch ✪$69; half day coastal kayaking $33.

FNQ Fishing Adventures, ✆4068 9000. Half day ✪$60; full day $110. Also sightseeing tours with crocodile and bird spotting.

Jump the Beach Skydiving, ✆1800 638 005 (bookings). From ✪$228-308.

RnR Rafting Tully River, ✆4051 7777. Full day rafting 8am-5pm, barbecue lunch, buffet dinner, ✪$123.

South Mission Beach Boat Hire, ✆0419 651 288 (mobile). Dinghy hire, ✪$30 for the first two hours, $10 for each additional hour.

Mission Beach Dive and Tackle, Shop 4, The Hub Shopping Centre, Porters Promenade, ✆4068 7294, offers bicycle hire.

Golfing enthusiasts can play rounds at the *El Arish Country Club*, Bruce Highway, El Arish, ✆4068 5140.

For a game of squash, head to *Mission Fitness* at the Gymnasium Mission Trade Centre, Unit 7, ✆4088 6555.

TOURS AND CRUISES

Dunk Island Jet Ski Tours, ✆4068 8699. A unique way to circumnavigate Dunk Island, ✪$180.

Friendship Cruises, Clump Point Jetty, Mission Beach, ✆4068 7262. Great Barrier Reef Cruise, adults ✪$66, chidren $33.

Mission Beach Dive Charters, ✆1800 700 112. Various dives and locations, from ✪$95-325.

Mission Beach Nature Tours, ©4068 8582. Canoe trip through the wet tropics rainforest, 8.30am-3.30pm, adults ✪$65, children $35, under 10 years $10.
Mission Beach Rainforest Treks, ©4068 7028. Guided rainforest walks, morning (adults ✪$28, children $14) and night ($18) tours.
Quickcat Cruises, ©1800 654 242. Dunk Island (adults ✪$26, children $15) and Outer Barrier Reef (adults $122, children $61), 10am-5pm.
Cardwell Air Charters, ©4066 8468. 5 flights, various locations, from ✪$35 to $229 for adults.

TULLY

Map D
Population 3100

LOCATION AND CHARACTERISTICS

With a population of around 3000, Tully is set at the foot of Mt Tyson, and is the centre of a large sugar cane and banana growing region. The Tully River rapids provide some very fine whitewater rafting and canoeing, and there is plenty of fishing for enthusiasts.

It should be noted that Tully has the highest annual rainfall in Australia (along with Innisfail) of around 3700mm. There is a definite Wet Season which begins in December and peaks in March. During this period it can rain every day, and sometimes all day. People intending to spend their holiday on either Dunk or Bedarra Islands should keep this in mind, since the paradise appeal of tropical islands is somewhat diminished when the rain just doesn't stop.

HOW TO GET THERE

By Rail

The Queenslander and Sunlander stop in Tully en route to Cairns, ©132 235.

By Coach

Greyhound Pioneer, ©13 2030, and McCaffertys, ©13 1499, use the Bruce Highway on their northbound/southbound journey to/from Cairns.

Townsville

By Car

Tully is on the Bruce Highway 106km north of Ingham, 222km north of Townsville, and 152km south of Cairns.

VISITOR INFORMATION

The Tully Information Centre, is on the Bruce Highway in Tully, ✆4068 2288.

ACCOMMODATION AND SERVICES

Tully, Bruce Highway, ✆4068 2233. 22 units, licensed restaurant, 9-hole golf course, undercover parking - ✪$56-65.

Googarra Beach Caravan Park, Tully Heads Road, ✆4066 9325. 50 sites, barbecue, pool - powered sites ✪$12 for two, cabins $36-40 for two.

Tully Heads Van Park, 56 Taylor Street, Tully Heads, ✆4066 9260. 40 sites, barbecue, pool - powered sites ✪$13 for two, cabins $35 for two, on-site vans $25 for two.

Eating Out

For a bite out, there is the *Raging Thunder Cafe*, on the Bruce Highway, Tully, ✆4068 3196.

POINTS OF INTEREST

Between June and November, tours of the **Sugar Mill** can be arranged through the information centre, ✆4068 1222. They begin at 10am, 11am, 1pm and 3pm, and cost ✪$7 per person, $18 for families.

The **Kareeya State Forest** is accessible via a spectacular drive up the Tully River gorge.

The **Tully Country Club**, Pratt Street, Tully ✆4068 1236, is an option for keen golfers.

TOURS

Raging Thunder Adventures, 52 Fearnley Street, Cairns, ✆4030 7900 or ✆4030 7990 (reservations), offer rafting on the Tully River. An all day tour includes pick-up at local accommodation, lunch, dinner and 5 hours of action - ✪$143, departing Mission Beach at 8am and returning 5pm. Tours also depart Port Douglas, Townsville and Cairns at

Townsville

earlier times. Raging Thunder also have Barron River rafting, Heli Raft, Jetboat, Bungy, kayaking, ballooning and adventure holiday packages, as well as combinations of all these.

CARDWELL

Map D
Population 8,800

LOCATION AND CHARACTERISTICS

Cardwell is a fishing village situated between the mountains and the sea. It is in the middle of a natural wonderland, with world heritage rainforests, waterfalls, swimming holes, wilderness tracks, whitewater rafting, canoeing, crabbing, fishing and prawning. The Cardwell lookout offers panoramic coastal views and there are very scenic drives to Murray Falls, Blencoe Falls, the Edmund Kennedy National Park, Dalrymple's Gap Track and Cardwell Forest.

Cardwell is also the gateway to Hinchinbrook Island, the world's largest Island National Park.

HOW TO GET THERE

By Rail

The Queenslander and Sunlander stop in Cardwell en route to Cairns, ✆13 2235.

By Coach

Greyhound Pioneer, ✆13 2030, and McCaffertys, ✆13 1499, pass through Tully on the Bruce Highway, stopping at the Cardwell Transit Centre.

By Car

Cardwell is on the Bruce Highway, about half-way between Tully and Ingham.

VISITOR INFORMATION

For tourist information, contact the Development Bureau of Hinchinbrook & Cardwell Shires, 77 Townsville Road, Ingham, ✆4776 5381.

Townsville

ACCOMMODATION AND SERVICES

Sunrise Village & Leisure Park, 43 Marine Parade, ✆4066 8550. 28 units, licensed restaurants (closed Sunday), undercover parking, pool, spa - ✪$60. Also has powered sites ✪$15 for two, villas $50-55 for two, cottages $40-55 for two, cabins $35.

Aquarius Motel and Holiday Units, 25 Bruce Highway, 4066 8755. 5 units, undercover parking, pool, spa - ✪$50-65.

Lyndoch Motor Inn, 215 Victoria Street, ✆4066 8500. 19 units, barbecue, licensed restuarant (closed Sunday), transfers, pool - ✪$50.

Marine, Victoria Street, ✆4066 8662. 8 units, licensed restaurant (closed Sunday) - ✪$37.

Caravan Parks

Kookaburra Holiday Park, 175 Bruce Highway, ✆4066 8648. 31 sites, barbecue, pool - powered sites ✪$13-15, cabins $80, units $55, on-site vans $32, bunkhouse $15.

Pacific Palms Caravan Park & Cabins, Bruce Highway, ✆4066 8671. 34 sites, unlicensed restaurant, kiosk, pool - powered sites ✪$13 for two, cabins $50 for two, bunkhouses $12 for one.

There is a **Youth Hostel** at 175 Bruce Highway, Cardwell, ✆4066 8648, with 28 rooms at ✪$18 per adult per night, twin share.

Eating Out

If you wish to eat out in Cardwell, there are a number of options, including *Beach Hut*, 93 Victoria Street, ✆4066 8080; *Muddies*, 219 Victoria Street, ✆4066 8907; and *Edward Kennedy*, 43 Marine Parade, ✆0417 771 975.

Local Transport

If you require local transport, Cardwell Taxis, ✆4066 8955, operate services in the area.

POINTS OF INTEREST

Edmund Kennedy National Park, nestles into the coastline about 4km north of the township. Its features a range from mangrove swamps to open woodland to pristine rainforest. There is a 3km walking track, with wooden boards and bridges for an easy stroll, which serves as the best and safest way to view the region.

> The **Cardwell Forest Drive**, is a 9km route that takes in outstanding coastal views, Attie Creek, safe swimming holes, Dead Horse Creek, Spa Pool, and barbecue picnic areas. Allow a full day to appreciate the sights and leisure opportunities along the way.
>
> Nearby natural wonders include **Tully Gorge** and **Dalrymple's Gap**, as well as the **Falls**: Murray, Blencoe and Wallaman (Australia's highest single-drop falls at 305m).
>
> For directions and conditions regarding each of these locations, contact the Development Bureau, ✆4776 5381.

Although it has plenty of attractive features itself, Cardwell is typically considered the gateway to Hinchinbrook Island (*see separate entry*).

Hinchinbrook Adventures & Ferries, Port Hinchinbrook Marina, Bruce Highway Cardwell, ✆4066 8270, offer cruises from Cardwell to Hinchinbrook Island, including lunch, morning tea, rainforest walks and 5 hours to explore the beauty of the island before returning. The cruise and tour costs are ✪$69 adults and $35 children.

Cardwell Air Charters, 22 Winter Street, ✆4066 8468, have various scenic flights over rainforest and reef.

PALUMA

Map D

LOCATION AND CHARACTERISTICS

61km (38 miles) north of Townsville, and 40km (25 miles) south of Ingham on the Bruce Highway, the Mount Spec Road turns towards the mountains of the Paluma Range, following the southern boundary of Mount Spec National Park. The road was built mainly by hand during the Great Depression.

Townsville

ACCOMMODATION AND SERVICES

23km (14 miles) further on is secluded **Hidden Valley**, with cabin accommodation at 46 Hidden Valley Road, including licensed facilities and a swimming pool, ✆4770 8088.

POINTS OF INTEREST

7km along the road lies **Little Crystal Creek**, with picnic, barbecue and toilet facilities, and deep pools for swimming.

18km (11 miles) from the highway, at about 900m (2953 ft) is **McClellands Lookout**, also with picnic, barbecue and toilet facilities. Near the lookout is **Paluma Village**, with its Ivy Cottage Tea-rooms, ✆4770 8533.

Also worth a visit is **Paluma Rainforest House** in Lennox Crescent, ✆4770 8560.

ISLAND RESORTS

There are hundreds of islands in the bays of Magnetic North, many are ancient mountain tops, others are coral atolls. For tourists wishing to island-hop in comfort, small high-quality resorts have been built on Orpheus, Hinchinbrook, Dunk and Bedarra Islands. Many of the other islands are uninhabited, although some offer restricted camping facilities, ✆3227 8187.

DUNK ISLAND

Map D

LOCATION AND CHARACTERISTICS

Dunk Island, across the bay from Mission Beach, is mostly National Park land, but there is one luxury resort. The island is shaped by rolling hills and deep valleys. It is home to the famous Ulysses butterfly.

Dunk Island is also part of the Family group of islands, and its Aboriginal name is Coonanglebah which means "isle of peace and plenty". Captain Cook named it Dunk after Lord Montague Dunk, the Earl of Sandwich, who was the First Lord of the Admiralty at the time.

Townsville

It is the largest island in the group and is sometimes called the Father of the Family Group (Bedarra is the Mother). The island's area is 10 sq km, but 7.3 sq km is national park. The Wet Season, when it is best not to visit, lasts from December to the end of March.

Cook recorded that Aborigines on these islands stood in groups and watched the *Endeavour* sail past, but they have long gone from the area. The earliest long term European resident was E.J. Banfield, who lived there from 1897 to 1923. He was a journalist on *The Townsville Daily Bulletin* when his doctor told him to slow down and take it easy, or face the consequences. So he and his wife decided to get back to nature and live on Dunk, where they were apparently very happy. When he wasn't tending his garden, Banfield wrote articles for his old newspaper, or worked on his books - *Confessions of a Beachcomber* (1908), *My Tropic Isle* (1911), *Tropic Days* (1918) and *Last Leaves from Dunk Island* (1925), the last published after his death.

The Banfields' house became part of a small resort that was opened in 1934 by Spenser Hopkins, a friend of theirs, but a year later that part of the island was sold with Hopkins only keeping the section where the Artists' Colony is today.

During the Second World War a radar station was set up on Mt Kootaloo and proved its worth during the Battle of the Coral Sea. Its remains can still be seen.

Dunk is very much a family resort and it has some good high tide beaches, but at low tide they are too shallow and have a lot of weeds. The island doesn't seem to have a significant problem with box jellyfish, but it is wise to keep an eye out during the November-March period.

There are 13km of walking tracks, and the 10km walk around the island rates among the best of any on the Barrier Reef islands.

Townsville

HOW TO GET THERE

By Air

Sunstate Airlines, ©13 1313, have flights to Dunk from Townsville and Cairns. Both flights take 45 minutes.

By Sea

Water taxis from Mission Beach to Dunk are operated by Dowd's Coaches & Water Taxi, © 4068 8968, and Mission Beach/Dunk Island Water Taxi, © 4068 8310.

VISITOR INFORMATION

Contact the Dunk Island Resort directly on ©4068 8199, visit the website at ☞www.dunkislandresort.com or email an information request at ✉visitors@greatbarrierreef.aus.net

ACCOMMODATION AND SERVICES

Dunk Island Resort, Dunk Island, ©4068 8199 - all inclusive rates are ✿$340-520 per double, per day.

The Resort accommodation consists of 148 rooms divided into four categories: Bayview Suites (4-star); Beach Front Units (3-star); Garden Cabanas (3-star); and Banfield Units (3-star).

Resort facilities are: live entertainment, restaurant, brasserie, cocktail bar, games room, two swimming pools, spa, tennis courts, laundry/ironing, Kids' Club, babysitting, snorkelling, catamaran sailing, parasailing, sailboarding, fishing, cricket, waterskiing, horse riding, golf, archery, tube rides, clay shooting, squash, Barrier Reef cruises and air tours, cruising and coral viewing, SCUBA diving, tandem skydiving, beach volleyball and EFTPOS.

Unit facilities are: tea/coffee making facilities, refrigerator, colour TV, in-house movies, IDD/STD telephone, radio, air-conditioning, ceiling fans, daily cleaning service, balcony or verandah, and interconnecting rooms.

Tariffs for one night per person/twin share are:

Banfield -   ✿$272 (child sharing with 2 adults - $40)
Beachfront - ✿$250 (child - as above)

Garden Cabana - ✪$212 (child - as above)

Bayview - ✪$176 (child - as above).

Note that a full breakfast is included in the daily rate.

Additional to the tariffs are: Artists' Colony visits, clay target shooting, game fishing, glass bottom boat tours, golf clinics, horse riding, massage therapist, nature walks and rainforest tours, outboard dinghies, reef cruises, scuba diving and lessons - resort and accredited courses and dive trips to the Great Barrier Reef, sunset cruises, tandem skydiving, tennis clinics, waterskiing.

Reservations can be made with the Resort over the phone, or online at the website listed under *Visitor Information* above.

Credit cards accepted: Visa, MasterCard, Bankcard, Diners Club, American Express.

Camping

Camping is permitted on the Foreshore reserve, and information and bookings can be obtained from the National Park Campsite, ✆4068 8199.

Fees are moderate and facilities include picnic tables, toilets, drinking water and showers. No fires are permitted.

Campers and day trippers are welcome to hire the Resort's equipment.

POINTS OF INTEREST

Bruce Arthur's Artists' Colony

Situated just beyond the Resort garden, the colony's longest term resident is former Olympic wrestler Bruce Arthur, who produces large and beautiful tapestries. He and his cohorts lease the land, and have an open house ⏰10am-1pm between Thursday and Sunday (small entry fee) when they chat about the island and their projects, and present their work for sale.

Diving

The Great Barrier Reef is an hour away by *Quickcat*, the high-speed catamaran, and there are four reefs to dive: Beaver, Farquharson, Yamacutta and Potter. They have some of the best coral and marine life on the Reef, and feature feeding stations, coral walls, caves, caverns and gardens. Trips to Beaver Reef include glass bottom boat, semi-submersible rides, lunch and onboard dive instruction.

All diving needs on Dunk are catered for by very experienced instructors. Training is available to international levels (PADI & NAUI) in a variety of courses from beginners to most experienced, including: Open Water Course, Advanced Rescue, Divemaster and specialist courses like night diving. Only the very latest equipment is available for hire at reasonable rates.

BEDARRA ISLAND

Map J

LOCATION AND CHARACTERISTICS

Part of the Family Group of Islands, Bedarra lies about 6km south of Dunk Island and about 5km offshore. It is privately-owned and is shown on marine charts as Richards Island.

Bedarra has an area of one square kilometre, and is a rainforest with natural springs and plenty of water. It has some very good sandy beaches. Note that it has a very definite Wet Season from December to the end of March, when it can rain every day and sometimes all day.

Originally occupied by Aborigines, the island was purchased by Captain Henry Allason from the Queensland Land Department for £20, and they threw in Timana Island for good luck. He sold Bedarra to Ivan Menzies, in the 1920s, for £500, and it then passed through several pairs of hands until it reached Dick Greatrix and Pierre Huret, who established gardens at the sandspit end. A section of the island had been sold to Australian artist Noel Wood in 1936, and another artist John Busst, leased the south-east corner. His home became the Plantation Resort (Bedarra Bay), and in 1947, Geatrix and Huret sold out to him.

There is a walking track from Bedarra Bay to the resort, which is in fact the only walking track.

Townsville

HOW TO GET THERE

By Sea

Bedarra Island is reached via Dunk Island. The boat connects with flights to/from Dunk, and the water taxis between Dunk Island and the mainland. Enquire when making a reservation.

VISITOR INFORMATION

The Bedarra Island Resort can be contacted on, ✆4068 8233. There is a web page at ☞www.bedarraisland.com with an email address at ✍visitors@greatbarrierreef.aus.net

ACCOMMODATION AND SERVICES

Bedarra Island Resort is on the eastern side of the island. It has 15 villas with 5-star ratings.

Resort facilities are: restaurant, cocktail lounge, swimming pool, spa, floodlit tennis court, laundry service, dinghies with outboards, sailboarding, snorkelling, fishing equipment, EFTPOS.

Villa facilities are: bathroom with bath, hair dryer and bath robes, queen size beds, refrigerator, mini bar, air-conditioning, ceiling fans, radio, telephone IDD/STD, daily cleaning service, beach towels, writing desk, separate living area, colour TV, video cassette recorder and private balcony.

Tariff for one night per person/twin share is ✪$680, which includes accommodation, all meals, drinks (including alcohol) and most activities.

Note that children under 16 years are not accepted at the Resort, and that maximum villa occupancy is 3 people.

Reservations can be made online at the website listed above, or over the phone.

Credit cards accepted: Visa, MasterCard, Bankcard, Diners Club, American Express.

POINTS OF INTEREST

Activities which are not included in the tariff are: Great Barrier Reef trips, boutique/shop, float plains, game fishing charters, hair salon (available on Dunk Island), private boat charters, sailing charters.

Townsville

Scuba Diving, Great Barrier Reef

Townsville

HINCHINBROOK ISLAND

Map D

LOCATION AND CHARACTERISTICS

Hinchinbrook is the world's largest island national park, with over 45,000ha (393 sq km) of tropical rainforests, mountains, gorges, valleys, waterfalls and sandy beaches. It is one of the most beautiful tropical islands in the world and offers some of the best bushwalking in Australia. A magnificent jagged mountain range drops to warm seas and coral reefs, dominating the skyline. The rainforests offer spectacular views.

The island is separated from the mainland by Hinchinbrook Channel, a narrow mangrove-fringed strip of water that is very deep. From further out at sea, the channel cannot be seen, and in fact, when Captain Cook sailed past he did not record the presence of an island.

Aborigines lived on the island and remains of their fish traps can be seen near the Scraggy Point camp site.

The best walk on any of the Great Barrier Reef islands is the three to four day walk along the eastern side of Hinchinbrook, but it is strongly recommended that information be obtained from the National Parks and Wildlife Service in Cardwell (near the jetty), ©4066 8601, before setting out. They can advise you on facilities on the island, give tips for climbing the mountains and protecting your supplies from the local wildlife, and issue permits for camping.

Remember that marine stingers may be around in the October-May period, and that crocodiles may be found in channel waters and estuaries.

HOW TO GET THERE

By Sea

Access is via boat from Cardwell. You can use Hinchinbrook Adventures & Ferries, Port Hinchinbrook Marina, Bruce Highway Cardwell, ©4066 8270.

VISITOR INFORMATION

For further information, contact the Development Bureau of Hinchinbrook & Cardwell Shires, 77 Townsville Road, Ingham, ©4776 5381. Alternatively, call the Island Resort on ©4066 8585. Updated information is provided at ☞www.hinchinbrookferries.com.au

ACCOMMODATION AND SERVICES

Hinchinbrook Island Resort, ©4066 8585, is a small resort located at Cape Richards to the north of the island.

It houses guests in 3 cabins and 15 treehouse units, all with their own bathrooms, tea/coffee making facilities and a refrigerator. The cabins have two bedrooms, and the newer treehouses have one or two. There is no TV or radio on the island, and only one telephone.

There is a licensed restaurant, a bar, a barbecue near the swimming pool, canoes, snorkelling gear, surf skis, fishing equipment, shop and a lending library. There is almost nothing in the way of night life, and

Townsville

even during the day there is not much organised activity. Hinchinbrook is the place to really 'get away from it all'.

Tariffs for one night are:

Cabins -   ✪$225 single, $450 double.

Treehouse Units - ✪$315 single, $630 double.

These rates include all meals and use of most of the equipment (except those requiring power).

Camping

The island has limited camping at ✪$3.50 per person per night (permit required, ✐4066 8601).

Macushla Camping Area - patrols, picnic tables, shelter shed, toilets, fires prohibited. Walking tracks, ocean swimming beaches, fishing spots, rainforest areas.

Goold Island - patrols, picnic tables, shelter shed, toilets, fires prohibited. Fishing and swimming.

ORPHEUS ISLAND

Map J

LOCATION AND CHARACTERISTICS

This island is mostly national park, but has a secluded resort at one end. Orpheus Island is encircled by wide beaches and a warm shallow sea. A fringe reef possesses a rich variety of marine life and provides excellent diving.

Orpheus Island has an area of 14 sq km and is the second largest in the Palm Island group. There are ten main islands in the group, but eight of them are Aboriginal reservations and permission must be obtained to visit. Orpheus is National Park while Pelorus, the other island not part of the reserve, is Crown Land.

The island is 80km north of Townsville and roughly 20km off Lucinda Point near Ingham. It was named in 1887, after the HMS *Orpheus* - the largest warship in Australia, which sank off New Zealand in 1863 with the loss of 188 lives. Orpheus is long and narrow and its fringing reef is probably the best of all the resort islands. It is heavily wooded and is home to a large population of wild goats. The goats were introduced many years ago as food for people who might be shipwrecked on the island, but they have obviously not been needed and have multiplied to the point where they are causing some problems.

There are a few beaches on the island, although some, such as Hazard Bay and Pioneer Bay, are only suitable for swimming at high tide. When the tide is out they become wading pools. Mangrove Bay and Yankee Bay are good places to swim at low tide.

As far as bushwalks are concerned, there is a shortage of them on this island. One traverses up to Fig Tree Hill, and the other winds from Hazard Bay through a forest to Picnic Bay.

There is a Marine Research Station, part of James Cook University, at Little Pioneer Bay, and it is engaged in breeding clams, both giant and other species, and transplanting them to other reefs where there is a shortage of them through overgathering. It is possible to visit the station, but prior arrangements should be made by contacting the station manager, ✆4777 7336.

The zoning for most of the water around Orpheus is Marine National Park B, although part of the south-west coast is zoned 'A'. So limited line fishing is allowed in the 'A' part, but collecting shells or coral is strictly forbidden.

HOW TO GET THERE

By Air
Daily flight by seaplane from Townsville with Nautilus Aviation, ✆4725 6056. Return air fares are ❂$310 from Townsville and $500 from Cairns. You must book when you make a resort reservation.

VISITOR INFORMATION
The number for the resort is, ✆4777 7377. The web page is ☞www.orpheusisland.com with an email facility at:
✉ reserv@greatbarrierreef.aus.net

ACCOMMODATION AND SERVICES

The *Orpheus Island Resort*, ©4777 7377, has 31 rooms that are rated 4-star.

Resort facilities are: restaurant, cocktail bar, lounge, barbecue area, entertainment, games room, tour desk, recreation room with television, gym equipment, two swimming pools, spa, boutique, tennis court, waterskiing, windsurfers, catamarans, snorkelling, paddleboards, boat charter, SCUBA diving, canoes, picnic lunches and laundry.

Room facilities are: private bathrooms, hairdryer, bathrobes, tea/coffee making facilities, refrigerator, mini bar, ceiling fans, radio/music, air-conditioning, non-smoking rooms, iron and a daily cleaning service.

The following tariffs are for one night per person/twin share:

Beachfront Terrace -　　　✪$450
Beachfront Studio -　　　　✪$540
Beachfront Bungalow -　✪$605
Hillside Villa -　　　　　　✪$630

These rates include all meals, snacks and most activities. Not included are those activities that require power. People under 15 years of age are not accepted at the Resort. Day trippers are not allowed in either.

Reservations can be made through the Resort or online. Credit cards accepted: American Express, Bankcard, MasterCard, Diners Club, Visa.

Camping

Camp sites are found at Pioneer Bay and Yankee Bay. They are patrolled, and have picnic tables, toilets and drinking water. For further information and booking, get in touch with the Rainforest and Reef Centre, Bruce Highway, Cardwell, ©4066 8601, or call Naturally Queensland on ©3227 8187.

Campers cannot buy meals at the Resort, and fires are not permitted on the island, so if you are intending to camp bring all your provisions, including water and a fuel stove.

POINTS OF INTEREST

As mentioned previously, Orpheus has some of the best fringing reef of all the islands, and good reefs are also found off Pelorus Island to the north and Fantome Island to the south. The Resort dive shop offers local dives and diving courses, but remember that these activities are not included in the Resort tariff.

There are many opportunities for bush walking and rainforest study, and snorkelling, as always, remains popular.

MAGNETIC ISLAND

Map D
Population 2200

LOCATION AND CHARACTERISTICS

Magnetic lies 8km across Cleveland Bay from Townsville, fifteen minutes by catamaran. It is roughly triangular in shape and has an area of 52 sq km.

With 16 beaches, plenty of reasonably-priced places to stay, and an ideal climate, this is one of the most popular islands on the Reef.

The island's first visitor was Captain Cook in 1770, and he declared it Magnetic Island, believing that it had interfered with his compass. Magnetic's first European settlers were timber cutters at Nelly Bay in the early 1870s. A permanent settlement was not established until 1887 when Harry Butler and his family arrived at Picnic Bay. It was these people who began the tourist industry on the island and their story is told in *The Real Magnetic* by Jessie Macqueen, who was also one of the early settlers. At the end of the century Robert Hayles built a hotel at Picnic Point and introduced a ferry service to the island on an old Sydney Harbour ferry, *The Bee*. The island now has a permanent population of more than 2200 people, and draws millions of holiday-makers.

It is one of the largest islands on the Great Barrier Reef, and 70 percent of it is National Park. A high spine of mountains covered by forests of eucalypts and wattles, and strewn with granite boulders, runs across the island. Below the peaks lie sheltered white beaches, rocky coves and coral reefs.

More than 22km (14 miles) of walking tracks lead over and around hills to secluded coves and quiet bays. The four small settlements of Picnic Bay, Nelly Bay, Arcadia and Horseshoe Bay offer a plentiful range of services for the visitor. You will also find an aquarium and a koala sanctuary.

Box jellyfish are present around Magnetic between October and April, so during this time it is wise to swim only in the netted areas at Picnic Bay and Alma Bay.

The north coast of Magnetic is zoned Marine Park B, so fishing is not permitted.

There are quite a few good diving locations on the island's southern and eastern shores.

HOW TO GET THERE

By Sea

Access is by cruises departing several times a day from Townsville. Sunferries, ©4771 3855, have a high-speed catamaran offering family packages for the 25-minute trip to Magnetic Island. Return fares start from ✪$14 adults, $7 children and $29 for families.

Magnetic Island Car & Passenger Ferry, Ross Street, South Townsville, ©4772 5422, run a car ferry to Arcadia from the south side of Ross Creek, but unless you are staying on the island for an extended period, a car is not really necessary.

VISITOR INFORMATION

For details about other attractions on the island, contact either the Magnetic Island Tourist Information Bureau and Central Booking Office, 26 The Grove, Nelly Bay, ©4778 5596, or the Magnetic Island Holiday and Information Centre in Picnic Bay Mall, ©4778 5155. Between them, they know everything there is to know about Magnetic Island, and have some helpful brochures. They can advise on your tour

Townsville

bookings, accommodation, vehicle hire, travel arrangements and even the best way to climb Mt Cook (497m).

There is a good website at ☞www.magnetic-island.com.au

ACCOMMODATION AND SERVICES

There is a wide variety of accommodation including hotels, motels, luxury resorts, self contained holiday units, flats, backpacker hostels and camping facilities. Most accommodation is either beachfront, or close to it. The area code for Queensland is (07).

Hotels/Motels

Magnetic Island International Hotel, Mandalay Avenue, ✆4778 5200 or ✆1800 079 902 (toll free). 80 units, licensed restaurant, gym, tennis, pool - ✪$170 room, $200 suite.

Tropical Palms Inn, 34 Picnic Street, Picnic Bay, ✆4778 5076. 14 units, pool - ✪$63-75 a double.

Arcadia Hotel Resort, 7 Marine Parade, Arcadia, ✆4778 5177. 27 rooms, licensed restaurant, swimming pool, spa - ✪$60-80 a double.

Magnetic Island Tropical Resort, Yates Street, Nelly Bay, ✆4778 5955. 30 units, licensed restaurant, spa, pool - ✪$45-84.

Self-Contained Units/B&B

Arcadia

Champagne Apartments, 38 Marine Parade, ✆4778 5002. 11 units, secure parking, barbecue, spa bath, pool - ✪$120-140.

Magnetic Haven, 7 Rheuben Terrace, ✆4778 5824. 7 units, playground, undercover parking, heated pool, spa - ✪$70-140.

Dandaloo Gardens, 40 Hayles Avenue, ✆4778 5174. 8 units, barbecue, playground, pool - ✪$70-85.

Island Magic Apartments, Armand Way, ✆4778 5077. 6 units, barbecue, undercover parking - ✪$70-85.

Marshalls Bed & Breakfast, 3 Endevour Road, Arcadia Bay, ✆4778 5112. 4 rooms - ✪$55 a double.

Magnetic Retreat, 11 Rheuben Terrace, ✆4778 5357. 7 units, undercover parking, transfers, pool, spa - ✪$50-80.

Townsville

Magnetic North Holiday Apartments, 2 Endevour Road, ✆4778 5647. 6 units, playground, undercover parking - ✪$85-100.

Wongalee, 17 McCabe Crescent, ✆4778 5361. 1 flat, pool - ✪$55-60.

Nelly Bay

Island Leisure Resort, 4 Kelly Street, ✆4778 5002. 17 units, licensed cafe, transfers, tennis, gym, pool, spa - ✪$99.

Island Palms Resort, 13 The Esplanade, ✆4778 5571. 12 units, undercover parking, tennis half-court, pool, spa - ✪$85-100.

Palm View Chalets, 114 Sooning Street, Nelly Bay, ✆4778 5596. 10 chalets, undercover parking, pool - ✪$50-75 a double.

Horseshoe Bay & Picnic Bay

Sails on Horseshoe, 13 Pacific Drive, Horseshoe Bay, ✆4778 5117. 11 units, undercover parking, pool - ✪$159.

Magnetic Island Holiday Units, 16 Yule Street, ✆4778 5246. 6 units, barbecue, undercover parking, transfers, heated pool - ✪$60-70.

There is a **Youth Hostel**, *Geoff's Place*, at 40 Horseshoe Bay Road, Horseshoe Bay, ✆4778 5577 or ✆1800 255 577 (toll free), with 30 rooms at ✪$18 per adult per night, twin share.

Two other venues for budget accommodation are for budget accommodation are **Centaur Guest House**, 27 Marine Parade, Alma Bay ✆4778 568 or ✆1800 655 680 (toll free); and *Forest Haven*, 11 Cook Road, Arcadia, ✆4778 5153.

Eating Out

In addition to the restaurants you will find in a few of the hotel complexes, **Crusoe's Magnetic Island Restaurant** is at 5a The Esplanade, Picnic Bay, ✆4778 5480. Alternatively, there is a small shopping centre in Arcadia and a general store in Horseshoe Bay where you can get supplies and cook for yourself.

Local Transport

Magnetic Island Bus Service, 44 Mandalay Ave, ✆4778 5130, has a three hour tour with an all-day unlimited carousel bus trip around Magnetic Island and all its attractions, including a stop at Koala Park

Oasis. Buses meet arriving ferries and depart from Picnic Bay, but do not pick up from accommodation. Note that the charge for the tour does not include entry into the Koala Park. Fares are ✪$30 adults and $15 children.

You can rent a moke for a novel way of moving around the island: Magnetic Island Rent-a-Moke are at 4 The Esplanade, Picnic Bay, ✆4778 5377.

The area is also serviced by Magnetic Island Taxi, 25 Marine Parade, Alma Bay, ✆13 1008. They operate 18 hours per day, seven days a week with pick-up and wheelchair facilities, bookings, ferry connections, tours and sightseeing in air conditioned cars.

Road Runner Scooter Hire, 3/4 The Esplanade, Picnic Bay, ✆4778 5222. Single seat 50cc mopeds (scooter) hire. Open 7 days. Rates include helmet and free kilometres.

POINTS OF INTEREST

Picnic Bay

This is where the ferry docks, and where many people choose to stay. A lookout above the town offers some good views, and to the west is Cockle Bay and the wreck of the *City of Adelaide*, which went aground in 1916. To the east is Rocky Bay, and a lovely secluded beach.

Nelly Bay

There is a pleasant beach with shade and barbecue facilities. At low tide the reef is visible. Some graves are found at the end of Nelly Bay, and they mark the resting places of pioneers.

Arcadia

The next bay you come to is Geoffrey Bay, with a 400m low-tide reef walk that begins at the southern end of the beach. There's a signboard that marks the starting point.

The Arcadia Hotel Resort offers all kinds of entertainment for guests and visitors, but one that is strictly "Queensland-ish" happens every Wednesday at 8pm - **cane toad racing**. For the uninitiated, cane toads are repulsive creatures that were imported from Hawaii years and years ago to eat a bug that was causing trouble for sugar cane growers. When in Hawaii the toads loved the bug and couldn't get enough of it; once in Australia they couldn't have cared less about the bug, but found plenty of other things they did like to eat, and began to live happy and contented lives which, of course, resulted in more and more cane toads and eclipsed the initial problem of the bug.

Anyway, back to the races. The person in charge of the meeting catches at least twelve toads, paints a different coloured stripe on each of them and auctions them off to the highest bidders in the waiting crowd. The animals are then put into the middle of a circle and the first one to hop over the outside ring is declared the winner, and his 'owner' scoops the pool. At a 'serious' meeting this can make the owner several hundred dollars richer.

The **Arcadia Pottery Gallery** is 200m from the hotel at 44 Armand Way (Horseshoe Bay Road), ✆4778 5600, and it is ⏱open daily 9am-4pm. It displays and sells work from dozens of potters and is worth visiting even if you are not intending to buy.

Continuing around the island the next bay is Arthur Bay, where there are reef fish caves, then Florence Bay, a sheltered shady beach where you can visit **"The Forts"**. These are relics of World War II and consist of a command post and signal station, gun sites and an ammunition store. The views from here are fantastic.

Then there is Balding Bay which can only be reached by walking track or by sea, and around the point is Horseshoe Bay, home to the Koala Park Oasis, Horseshoe Bay Lagoon Environmental Park, water birds and a Mango farm. **The Koala Park Oasis**, in Pacific Drive, also has wombats, kangaroos, wallabies, emus and birds, and is ⏱open daily 9am-5pm. Admission is ✪$10 adult and $4 children, ✆4778 5260.

Further around is Five Beach Bay, which is only accessible by boat, and West Point, a very secluded area that people say has the best sunsets ever seen.

SPORT

There is a golf course at Picnic Bay, ✆4778 5188, and horse riding at Horseshoe Bay - *Blueys Horseshoe Ranch Trail Rides*, 38 Gifford Street, ✆4778 5109. ✪$45 for 2 hour bush and beach ride, $70 for half-day bush and beach (with morning tea). *Blueys* is ⏱open daily 7am-7pm.

Horseshoe Bay Watersports, 97 Horseshoe Bay Road, Horseshoe Bay, ✆4758 1336, offer beach hire for paraflying, water skiing, jet skiing, catamarans, aqua bikes, boats and motors, free stinger suits and waverunners. ⏱Open daily, weather permitting.

Diving

Comprehensive diving courses are available. Some include diving theory, meals, training, reef dives, and provide you with an internationally recognised certificate. Be aware you may require a doctor's certificate to prove your fitness level, and 2 passport photos. Those who are already certified divers, or who wish only to snorkel among the coral, can take either short trips out into the reef, or expeditions that last for days. Tanks and weight belts are usually provided but additional gear may have to be hired.

Pleasure Divers, Arcadia Resort Shop 2, Marina Parade, Alma Bay, ✆4778 5788, is a dive shop and dive school with scuba hire, snorkel hire, reef and island bookings, adventure bookings and Saturday night dives - from ✪$149 open Water PADI. ⏱Open daily 9am-4.30pm.

Alternatively, the *Magnetic Island Dive Centre* can be contacted on ✆4758 1399.

TOURS

Pure Pleasure Cruises, Great Barrier Reef Wonderland, 4 The Strand, Townsville, offer 9 hour tours from Townsville and Magnetic Island to Kelso Reef on the Wave Piercer 2001. The trip includes morning and afternoon tea, a tropical smorgasboard lunch, glass bottom coral viewing, swimming, snorkelling and scuba - ✪$110 adults, $55 children, ✆4721 3555 or ✆1800 079 797 (free call)

Adrenalin Jet Ski Tours, 89 Gifford Street, ✆4778 5533, take you around the island's coastal waters, with commentary.

Townsville

TOWNSVILLE

Map E

Population 140,000

Townsville is situated on the eastern coast of Australia, 1443km (897 miles) north of Brisbane.

CLIMATE

Average temperature: January max 31C (88F) - min 24C (75F) and high humidity; July max 25C (77F) - min 15C (59F). Average annual rainfall is 1194mm (47 ins) - wettest months January-March, with an average of 873mm (34 ins).

CHARACTERISTICS

The second largest city in Queensland and main commercial centre of northern Queensland, Townsville sprawls along the shores of Cleveland Bay and around the foot of Castle Hill. It offers not only easy access to the attractions of the Magnetic North and the Great Barrier Reef, but also all of the facilities of a major city.

Careful zoning has ensured that the city retains much of its original architecture and character. A walk around town will show you what makes North Queensland so different. Old wooden, highset houses stand everywhere, built to allow cooling breezes under the house and to provide a refuge during the heat of the day. In the gardens, mango, paw paw and banana trees seem exotic to the visitor, but are the normal homegrown product of the Townsville backyard.

Townsville is also a busy port that services Mt Isa, southern cities and south-east Asia. It has two metal refineries and other industrial enterprises.

HOW TO GET THERE

By Air

Qantas, ©13 1313, and Ansett, ©13 1300, have flights to/from Adelaide, Alice Springs, Brisbane, Cairns, Darwin, Gold Coast, Hobart, Launceston, Melbourne, Newcastle, Perth and Sydney.

Ansett Airlines also have flights to/from Broome, Burnie, Devonport and Orpheus Island.

Sunstate Airlines, ✆13 1313, have flights to/from Brampton Island, Lizard Island, Mackay, Proserpine, Rockhampton and Thursday Island. Flight West, ✆1300 130 092, is another airline that services Townsville.

By Coach

Greyhound Pioneer, ✆13 2030, and McCaffertys, ✆13 1499, both stop at Townsville on their Brisbane-Cairns services.

By Rail

The Queenslander and the Sunlander services connect Townsville to both Brisbane and Cairns four times weekly, ✆13 2235. Sleeping berths and motor rail facilities are available.

By Road

From Brisbane along the Bruce Highway, 1443km (897 miles); from Brisbane along the inland route, 1505km (935 miles). Townsville is 374km south of Cairns.

The Flinders Highway connects Townsville with Mt Isa and Alice Springs.

It is important to listen to a local radio station for reports on road conditions during wet weather, as roads in northern Queensland are often cut during heavy rain.

VISITOR INFORMATION

The Townsville Enterprise Tourism Bureau is in Enterprise House, 6 The Strand, ✆4771 3061. There is also a Visitors Information Centre in Flinders Mall, ✆4721 3660, ◷open 9am-5pm Mon-Fri and 9am-1pm Sat-Sun.

ACCOMMODATION

Townsville has over 30 motels, hotels, guest houses, hostels and half a dozen camping grounds. Here is a selection with prices for a double room per night, which should be used as a guide only. The telephone area code is 07.

Townsville

Townsville

Sheraton Townsville Hotel & Casino, Sir Leslie Theiss Drive, ©4722 2333. 192 rooms, 16 suites, licensed restaurant, bars, swimming pool, spa, sauna, gym, tennis courts, casino - ✪$250.

Centra Townsville, Flinders Mall, ©4772 2477. 158 rooms, licensed restaurants, bars, gym, rooftop swimming pool - ✪$170.

Aquarius on the Beach Townsville, 75 The Strand, North Ward, ©4772 4255. 100 rooms, licensed restaurant (closed Sun), bistro, swimming pool - ✪$115-125.

South Bank Motor Inn, 23 Palmer Street, South Townsville, ©4721 1474. 94 units, 4 suites, licensed restaurant, cocktail bar, swimming pool, spa, undercover parking - ✪$90-110.

Castle Lodge, cnr Warburton & McKinley Streets, North Ward, ©4721 2290. 24 units, licensed restaurant (Mon-Sat), pool - ✪$85.

City Oasis Inn, 143 Wills Street, ©4771 6048 or ©1800 809 515 (toll free). 42 units, 2 suites, licensed restaurant, playground, pool, 2 spas - ✪$79-130.

Historic Yongola Lodge, 11 Fryer Street, ©4772 4633. 8 units, licensed restaurant, pool, next to *National Trust* restaurant - ✪$79-95.

Shoredrive, 117 The Strand, ©4771 6851. 30 units, unlicensed restaurant, pool - ✪$65.

Bessell Lodge, 38 Bundock Street, Belgian Gardens, ©4772 5055. 50 units, licensed restaurant, cocktail bar, live entertainment, barbecue - ✪$60-70.

Aitkenvale, 224 Ross River Road, Aitkenvale, ©4775 2444. 26 units, 2 suites, licensed restaurant, swimming pool, playground, undercover parking - ✪$58-62.

Hotel Allen, cnr Eyre & Gregory Streets, ©4771 5656. 45 units, 5 suites, pool - ✪$55.

Adobi, 86 Abbott Street, ©4778 2533 or ©4778 2745. 12 units, pool - ✪$45.

Caravan Parks

Sun City Caravan Park, 119 Bowen Road, ©4775 7733. 132 sites, pool, barbecue, playground - powered sites ✪$16 for two, on-site vans $30-35 for two, cabins $40 for two.

Magnetic Gateway Holiday Village, Bruce Highway, South Side, adjacent to Stuart Drive-in, ✆4778 2412. (No pets) 108 sites, barbecue, pool - powered sites ✪$15 for two, villas $45 for two.

Coonambelah Caravan Park, 547 Ingham Road, ✆4774 5205. (Pets on application) 75 sites - powered sites ✪$15 for two, on-site vans $28-35 for two, cabins $28-45 for two.

Town & Country Caravan Park, 16 Kings Road, ✆4772 1487. (No pets allowed) 72 sites, pool, barbecue, playground - powered sites ✪$14 for two, on-site vans $30 for two, cabins $45 for two.

EATING OUT

Townsville has many hotels serving counter lunches and takeaways, and some good restaurants. The international hotels have at least one restaurant, and the staff where you are staying can probably recommend a restaurant on the basis of price or cuisine. Following is a broad sample for all tastes and budgets.

Scirocco Cafe Bar & Grill, 61 Palmer Street, ✆4724 4508. Mediterranean and Asian cuisine, alfresco dining. Open Tues-Sat 6pm-midnight, and for lunch from midday-2pm, 10am-4pm on Sunday, closed Monday and Public Holidays.

The Pier Waterfront Restaurant & Bar, Sir Leslie Thiess Drive, ✆4721 2567. Licensed restaurant with waterfront views. Seafood and steak, light lunches served. Open midday-2pm for lunch and 6pm-midnight for dinner 7 days.

Covers Restaurant, 209 Flinders Street, ✆4721 4630. Open 6pm-midnight Mon-Sat and for lunch Wed-Fri, closed Sunday and Public Holidays.

Flutes Restaurant, 63 The Strand, ✆4721 1777. Operates 24 hours a day, 7 days, in the Best Western Motel.

Hong Kong Restaurant, 455 Flinders Street, West Townsville, ✆4771 5818. A-la-carte menu with home-style cooking a specialty. Open 5pm-8pm Mon-Sat and for lunch Mon-Fri, closed Sunday and Public Holidays.

Townsville

Townsville from the air

Wayne and Adeles Garden of Eating, 11 Allen Street, South Townsville, ✆4772 2984. Open 6.30-11pm Mon, Wed-Sat and Public Holidays, Sun 11am-3pm, closed Tuesday.

Metropole Hotel, 81 Palmer Street, South Townsville, ✆4771 4285. Seafood restaurant with gaming facilities and a beer garden in the complex. Open 24 hours, 7 days.

Taiping Chinese Restaurant, 350 Sturt Street, City, ✆4772 3619. A-la-carte, yum cha and buffet selections. Open midday-2pm and 5.30-midnight 7 days, closed Public Holidays.

Seagulls Resort, 74 The Esplanade, Belgian Gardens, ✆4721 3111. Open 6.30am-midnight every day.

Centra Townsville, Flinders Mall, ✆4772 2477. A-la-carte buffet menu and a cocktail bar. Open 7am-10pm every day.

Hogs Breath Cafe, 247 Flinders Street, ✆4771 5747. Open for lunch 11.30am-2.30pm and dinner 5.30pm-2.30am every day.

Pepperleaf at the Seaview, 56 The Strand, Townsville, ✆4771 5900.

McDonalds is on the corner of Flinders Mall and Denham Street. KFC is in the Nathan Plaza Stockland Shopping Centre. Pizza Hut is at 260 Ross River Road and on the corner of Charters Towers and Bayswater Roads, ✆13 1166.

ENTERTAINMENT

First and foremost in this category would have to be the:

Sheraton Townsville Hotel & Casino, Sir Leslie Theiss Drive, ©4722 2333. It was North Queensland's first licensed casino. Here you can try blackjack, the Sheraton wheels, two-up, roulette, keno, mini-dice, craps and mini baccarat. They also have video games and Sky Channel. To get the tourists in they offer a free courtesy bus service to most hotels and motels. The casino is ©open from noon to the early hours of the morning.

Townsville Civic Theatre is in 41 Boundary Street, South Townsville, ©4727 9013 or ©4727 9797 (box office), and can seat 1066 people. It offers culturally diverse programs.

The **Entertainment & Convention Centre**, ©4771 4000, on Entertainment Drive, is primarily for indoor sport, such as basketball, but if a big-name performer or band hits town, this is where the concert will be.

Fisherman's Wharf in Ogden Street has live entertainment seven nights a week, a restaurant, coffee shop and a bar.

If you are in the mood for dancing, head for Flinders Street where there is a night club, *Bullwinkles*, ©4771 5647.

For a pub night out try the *Great Northern Hotel* in 496 Flinders Street, ©4771 6191.

SHOPPING

Flinders Street Mall has several boutiques and specialty shops and *Northtown on the Mall*, ©4772 1566, but the big shopping centres are out of town.

At Aitkenville, 20 minutes from the city centre is *Stockland*, 310 Ross River Road, ©4779 6033, which has David Jones department stores as well as specialty shops. Nearby is *K-Mart Plaza*, Nathan Street, ©4779 9277, which has food shops and, of course, K-Mart.

The suburb of Pimlico has *Castletown*, 35 Kings Road, ©4772 1699, which has a variety of chain stores, including Target. The suburb of Kirwan has *The Willows*, Thuringowa Drive, ©4773 6333.

North Queensland's largest arts and crafts market is held in Flinders Mall every ☼Sunday 9am-1pm. Called *Cotters Market* it has pottery, jewellery, paintings, leadlighting, leatherwork, woodwork, crocheting and knitwear, original handicrafts, wooden toys, hats, homemade goodies, plants and preserves, islander crafts, timber, fishing lures, homemade chocolates, Devonshire teas, orchids, souvenirs, and seasonal fruit and vegies. What more could you want?

POINTS OF INTEREST

Castle Hill (286m - 938 ft) offers a panoramic view of Townsville. It is topped by an octagonal restaurant which commands a 260 degree view of the town and the bay. Nearby **Mount Stuart** is also an excellent vantage point.

Flinders Mall is virtually the heart of the city. It is a landscaped pedestrian mall with a relaxed atmosphere.

The **Perc Tucker Regional Gallery** is in the mall, ✆4727 9011, and it houses an extensive collection of national and regional art in an impressive building that was originally a bank. It is ☼open Mon-Thurs 10am-5pm, Fri 10-6pm, Sat-Sun 10am-2pm, and admission is free. Nearby **St Joseph's Cathedral** in Fryer Street, North Ward, ✆4772 1973, is a reflection of the architecture of the past.

The Strand, Townsville's sea promenade, has many parks including the Sister Kenny Park, and the Anzac Memorial Park with its Centenary Fountains, waterfall and bougainvillea gardens. Also along The Strand is the Tobruk Memorial Swimming Pool.

Queen's Gardens next to Queen's Park, encompasses Kissing Point and Jezzine Army Barracks. An all-tide rock swimming pool, a restaurant and a kiosk are also in the gardens.

The Town Common Environmental Park is a flora and fauna sanctuary where visitors may see some rare water fowl, including the primitive magpie goose. In the winter months, at the height of the dry season, as many as 3000 brolgas, along with up to 180 other species of bird, flock to the Common's salt-marsh lagoons and waterholes. The brolga is famous for its courting ritual, and the park provides

Townsville

visitors with an excellent opportunity to see this dance at close quarters. The park is ☺open daily 6.30am-6.30pm and barbecue facilities are available.

Great Barrier Reef Wonderland in Flinders Street East, is one of the most popular attractions in Townsville. It features the **Great Barrier Reef Aquarium**, ©4750 0891 - the world's largest living coral reef aquarium. Conceived and operated by the Great Barrier Reef Marine Park Authority, the aquarium includes a huge main tank containing a living coral reef, a smaller tank displaying sharks and other reef predators and an extensive area containing numerous display tanks, educational exhibits, a theatrette and a large touch-tank. You actually walk beneath the water through a transparent tunnel surrounded by hundreds of coral reef animals. Admission costs are ✪$14.80 for adults, $6.50 children and $35 for families. This very popular attraction is ☺open 9am-5pm.

Wonderland also houses: the operational headquarters of the Great Barrier Reef Marine Park Authority, the federal government agency responsible for safeguarding the Great Barrier Reef Marine Park (Reef HQ); a licensed restaurant featuring tropical cuisine; a shop with a variety of souvenirs and educational material; a post office; and an information centre with all you need to know about national parks, marine national parks, camping permits and locations, walking trails, and wildlife.

Townsville

An **Imax Theatre**, ©4721 1481 is close to the aquarium, at 86 Flinders Street. The theatre is dome-shaped and uses a special type of projection so that the image is projected above and around the audience - a fascinating experience. The theatre seats 200 people, including facilities for the handicapped.

The **Museum of Tropical Queensland**, 78-102 Flinders Street, ✆4726 0600, has recently undergone a complete transformation. The former museum has been expanded and modernised into a new and improved complex, opened in June 2000. It has an extensive array of exhibits, from the life-cycle of the world's largest moth to various Aboriginal crafts, and is worth a visit.

From the Wonderland ferry terminal there are cruises leaving for Magnetic Island and the Great Barrier Reef throughout the day. And while you are waiting to pick up your cruise, or the next show at the theatre, you can spend some time in the specialty shops in the complex.

Pangola Park, Spring Creek, ✆4782 9252, between Giru and Woodstock, is about 40 minutes' drive from Townsville. It has ideal swimming spots and adjoins a National Park with mountain streams and waterfalls. There is good bushwalking, picnic areas, barbecues, caravan and camping sites, a licensed kiosk, fishing spots, minibikes, and conducted horse and pony rides on weekends and public holidays. The park is ⊕open daily and an admission fee is charged. Camping and powered sites are available.

South of Townsville, in fact much closer to the town of Ayr, the wreck of the *Yongala* lies off Cape Bowling Green. A coastal steamer, she was bound for Cairns when a cyclone struck on March 14, 1911, and she went down with all hands - 121 people including officers and crew. The wreck was discovered in 1958, but has only been dived regularly since the 1980s.

Diving the *Yongala* is rated as one of the best wreck-dive experiences in the world.

The wreck is 110m long, and supports a system of hard and soft corals and many different marine animals including pelagics, stingrays, gropers, turtles and sea snakes. She lies in 30m of water with her funnel only 15m below the surface. The *Yongala* is protected by the Historic Shipwreck Act as a memorial to all who went down with her, so nothing may be taken from the ship. This is a temptation as there are dinner plates, knives, forks, and some evidence of human remains, but where they are they must stay. See the Diving section under *Sport* for operators who will take divers to the wreck.

SPORT

Swimming

There are three salt water mesh swimming enclosures, one at Rowes Bay, one at Pallarenda, and one next to the rock pool in Queen's Gardens. They provide safe sea swimming free from sharks, seastingers and other marine hazards.

Golf

Townsville Golf Club, Benson Street, Rosslea, ✆4779 0133. 27-hole championship course - equipment hire - ⏲open 6.30am-6pm, clubhouse open 10am-8pm.

Rowes Bay Golf Club, Cape Pallarenda Road, Pallarenda, ✆4774 1288. 18-hole par 72 course - equipment hire - ⏲open seven days.

Willows Golf Club, Nineteenth Avenue, Kirwan, ✆4773 4352 - 18-hole course - ⏲open daily.

Horse Riding

Ranchlands Equestrian School, 83 Hammond Way, Kelso, ✆4774 0124 - ⏲open week days and nights.

Saddle Sense Riding School, 95 Haynes Road, Jensen, ✆4751 6372 - trail rides and camping - ⏲open Wed-Sun.

Fishing/Yacht Charters

Tangaroa Cruises, 19 Crowle Street, Hyde Park ✆4772 2127. 50ft motor cruiser available for extended cruises, social outings, fishing and diving trips - support vessel.

True Blue Charters, 65 Gilbert Crescent, North Ward, ✆4771 5474. Charter boat for reef and game fishing, diving, snorkelling, island cruising - maximum 8 passengers - full boat charter - half day and other charters on request.

Townsville

Farr Better Yacht Charters, 76 Allen Street, South Townsville, ✆4771 6294. Yacht and boat charter - bare boat or with sail guide - *Hood* 23ft yacht and *Farr Star* 40ft yacht - sailing training (AF) - 7 days. Special weekend trips to Palm and Dunk Islands.

Diving

Diving courses are not cheap, and you should expect to pay at least ✪$400 for a comprehensive open water instruction program. If you are already a qualified diver, the cost for a guided dive is considerably less, and depends on the location and duration of the dive. Following are a few examples of companies operating in the area.

Mike Ball Dive Expeditions, 252 Walker Street, ✆4772 3022 - internationally acclaimed 5 star PADI dive centre providing PADI instruction from entry level to Dive career programs - expeditions to Yongala wreck and Coral Sea, also Cod Hole - ☀open Mon-Fri 8.45am-5pm, Sat 8.45am-noon.

The Dive Bell, 16 Dean Street, South Townsville, ✆4721 1155 - sport diving and dive shop - commercial diving school - diving trips to Yongala wreck and the reef - ☀open Mon-Fri 8.30am-5pm, Sat 9am-noon.

Pro-Dive Townsville, Great Barrier Reef Wonderland, Flinders Street, ✆4721 1760. PADI scuba diving school - 5 star Gold dive shop - charter boats, hire equipment, learn to dive - Yongala wreck dives (up to 3 days) - ☀open daily 9am-5pm.

Skydiving

Coral Sea Skydivers, Shop 3, 14 Plume Street, Townsville, ✆4772 4889. Tandem and accelerated free fall dives for beginners and experienced jumpers - souvenir videos, photos and certificates - Tandem Dives: 8,000 feet ✪$220; 12,000 feet $320 - Accelerated Free Fall Course: $450 - Complete Free Fall Course, including training and 12 jumps: $2,200.

TOURS

Detours, Shop 5, Great Barrier Reef Wonderland Complex, ✆4721 5977, offer the following trips.

Townsville

Tropical Rainforest and Waterfalls - Mt Specs National Park, Balgal Beach, Little Crystal Creek rainforest walk, Frosty Mango fruit farm - 8 hours - ✪$69 adults, $27 children - 9am Tues, Thurs, Sat.

The Real Outback - Charters Towers and outback country - 8 hours - ✪$69 adults, $27 children - 9am Wed & Sat.

Billabong Sanctuary - wildlife sanctuary - 4 hours - ✪$32 adult, $16 child (includes entrance fee) - 10am daily.

Tropical City Tour - more than 9 points of interest visited - 2 hours - ✪$24 adult, $8 child - 11am weekdays.

Night Tour - Castle Hill, Casino, Entertainment Centre - 1 hour - ✪$17 adults, $5 children - 6pm-7pm Mon-Thu May-Oct.

Hinchinbrook Island - coach to Cardwell, cruise to Hinchinbrook, self-guided walk - 12 hours - ✪$104 adults, $45 children - 6am Tues, Thu & Sun.

Dunk & Bedarra Islands - Mission Beach to Dunk Island to Bedarra Island, lunch, boom netting, tropical fruit tasting - ✪$98 adult, $45 child - 6am Thurs & Sun.

Raging Thunder, 52 Fearnlet Street, Cairns, ✆4030 7990. Although based in Cairns, this company has a 5-day tour that departs Townsville and takes in the best of the Tropical North. The highlight of day one is 5 hours of Tully River rafting then transfer to Cairns. Day two comprises a 5 hour reef cruise. Day three begins with a Hot Air Balloon flight above the Atherton Tablelands, a visit to Kuranda Markets, then a return trip to Cairns on the Skyrail. Day four is an exploration of Cape Tribulation and Daintree, including a Crocodile Cruise on the river. On day five you are taken to Fitzroy Island to relax or take the optional tour, then return later to Cairns.

The cost of the tour is ✪$475 per person, but you must arrange your own accommodation for the duration of the tour.

CRUISES

Coral Princess Cruises, Breakwater Terminal, Sir Leslie Thiess Drive, ✆4721 1673 or ✆1800 079 545 (free call), offer these trips.

Townsville

Townsville/Barrier Reef/Islands - 4 days/3 nights Barrier Reef and Island cruise - departs Townsville 1pm - calls at resorts, uninhabited islands and reef - from ✪$1183 per person twin share. 8 day/7 night cruise - combines 3 night Townsville with 3 night Cairns cruise - $1936 per person twin share.

Magnetic Island Ferry, Ross Street, South Townsville, ✆4772 5422, offer:
Cruise to Magnetic Island - open return ticket, free pick up from accommodation - bus or mokes available - ✪$14 adult, $7 child.

Magnetic Island Cruise/Bus - open duration, pick up from accommodation, cruise and bus tour of island with commentary, exploring and swimming - ✪$23 adult, $11.50 child.

Cruise/Moke Hire - return ferry fare with moke hire on the island - includes insurance and island map - ✪$27 per person.

Pure Pleasure Cruises, Great Barrier Reef Wonderland, 4 The Strand, Townsville, ✆4721 3555 or ✆1800 079 797 (freecall), offer a:
Kelso Outer Reef Tour - 50 nautical miles north to Kelso reef on the Wave Piercer 2000 - includes swimming, snorkelling, fishing, glass bottom boat, buffet lunch, morning/afternoon tea all inclusive, bar and diving extra - ✪$120 adult, $60 child - departs 9am daily.

SCENIC FLIGHTS

Townsville Aero Club, Townsville Aerodrome, Garbutt, ✆4779 2069. Aircraft charter, joy flights, aerial tours.

Inland Pacific Air, Townsville Aerodrome, Garbutt, ✆4775 3866 - twin engine aircraft charter 4 to 11 seats - 7 aircraft available including pressurised executive Cessna - available all hours to any destination. Also at Townsville Airport are *Nautilus Aviation*, ✆4725 6056, *Bluewater Aviation* ✆4725 1888, and *Magnetic North Aviation*, ✆4725 6227.

FESTIVALS

Pacific Festival is held each September/October, and lasts for 10 days.
   The Visitor Information Centre will advise on all current events at the time of your trip.

TOWNSVILLE TO MACKAY
HOME HILL AND AYR

Map J
Population 8600 and 3300 respectively.

LOCATION AND CHARACTERISTICS

The twin towns of Home Hill and Ayr are 90km (56 miles) south of Townsville on the Bruce Highway, and sit either side of the delta of the Burdekin River, slightly inland from the coast. The Burdekin is the main waterway of the Magnetic North, and its catchment area includes the mountains to the north and the goldfields to the west.

HOW TO GET THERE

By Coach

McCaffertys, ✆13 1499, and Greyhound Pioneer, ✆13 2030, service Ayr daily.

By Rail

The Ayr Railway Station is in Station Street, ✆4783 2214, for current schedules.

By Road

Both towns are conveniently located on the Bruce Highway, 90km south of Townsville.

VISITOR INFORMATION

The Burdekin Tourist Information Centre is in Plantation Park, on the Bruce Highway, Ayr, ✆4783 5988.

ACCOMMODATION AND SERVICES

Accommodation is limited and far from flash in both of these towns, but here is a sample guide.

Ayr

Country Ayr, 197 Queen Street, ✆4783 1700. 4 units, licensed restaurant (closed Sunday), undercover parking, pool - ✪$74-80.

Ayr Shamrock, 274 Queen Street, ©4783 1044. 10 units, undercover parking, pool - ✪$53.

Ayr Max Motel, 4 Edward Street, Bruce Highway North, ©4783 2033. 12 units, barbecue, undercover parking, pool, spa - ✪$50.

Tropical City Motor Inn, cnr MacMillan & McKenzie Streets, ©4783 1344. 16 units, licensed restaurant, undercover parking, room service, pool - ✪$48.

Caravan Parks

Silver Link Caravan Park, 34 Norham Road, ©4783 3933. 75 sites, barbecue, playground, kiosk, pool, spa - powered sites ✪$15 for two, villas $42 for two, cabins $35 for two, bunkhouses $28 for two.

Burdekin Cascades Caravan Park, 228 Queen Street, ©4783 1429. 42 sites, playground - powered sites ✪$14 for two, cabins $30 for two.

Eating Out

If you don't wish to eat at your motel, the *Burdekin Chinese Seafood Resturant* is at 110 Edward Street, ©4783 3444. There is also *Peppers on Queens*, 199 Queens Street, ©4783 1029 and *Charley's*, Queen Street, ©4783 4051.

Local Transport

You may require transport in the region, and in that case the Supreme Taxi Company can be contacted on ©4783 2244.

Home Hill

Burdekin Motor Inn, 14 Eighth Avenue, ©4782 1511. 14 units, licensed restaurant (closed Sunday-Thursday), undercover parking, room service, pool - ✪$50.

Caravan Park

Bartons Caravan Park, Eighth Avenue, ©4782 1101. 34 sites, playground - powered sites ✪$12 for two.

POINTS OF INTEREST

The **Ayr Nature Display**, 119 Wilmington Street, Ayr, ©4783 2189, has stunning displays ranging from reptiles to butterflies, birds to

Mackay

insects and fossils to shells. Admission is ✪$2.50 adults and $1 children, and the Nature display is ☉open 8am-5pm daily.

The river and its tributaries offer some of the best **freshwater fishing** for barramundi, grunter and bream in Australia, while the river delta and Alva Beach tempt the salt water fisherman with whiting, flathead and salmon. The Burdekin River is also the hub of other river-based activities from water skiing to picnicking.

The wreck of the SS *Yongala* lies 20km (12 miles) out to sea and is a fine diving site.

Cape Upstart National Park, some 70km (43 miles) from town, is an imposing granite headland rising from the sea.

CHARTERS TOWERS

Map J
Population 12,000

LOCATION AND CHARACTERISTICS

The Outback is just on the other side of the mountains. If you wish to divert from your coastal holiday for a while, the old gold rush town of Charters Towers can be reached 135km (84 miles) south-west of Townsville on the Flinders Highway. Now a town of 12,000 people, Charter Towers was once home to more than twice this number.

Three itinerant prospectors discovered gold in 1871, and between then and 1911, some seven million ounces of gold were taken from the region. The memories may be growing dim, but the town looks much the same as it did a century ago. Historic buildings line the streets and remnants of the gold mining era dot the surrounding countryside.

In recent years a few small scale operations recommenced, and some gold was extracted from the area.

HOW TO GET THERE
By Air

Charters Towers airport is serviced by small regional airlines, ©4787 3293.

By Rail

A railway network connects Townsville to Charters Towers. All travel arrangements and enquiries can be made through Traveland in Charters Towers, ✆4787 2622.

By Bus

Buses run daily from Townsville to Charters Towers.

By Road

Follow the Flinders Highway west from Townsville for 135km.

VISITOR INFORMATION

For more information contact the Charters Towers Dalrymple Tourist Information Centre, 74 Mosman Street, Charters Towers, ✆4752 0314. You can email them at ✉tourinfocentre@httech.com.au

ACCOMMODATION AND SERVICES

Charters Towers offers a wide range of accommodation in and around the city, from units to caravan parks, from modern hotels to original wooden hotels built during the gold rush. There is sufficient accommodation in this heritage town for a short stay, if you wish to take some time to view the restored historic buildings. The area code is (07).

Virginia Park Farm Stay, Flinders Highway, ✆4770 3125. 5 rooms, barbecue, undercover parking, tennis, horse riding - ✪$150 including meals.

Hillview, Flinders Highway, ✆4787 1973. 11 units, playground, undercover parking, pool - ✪$55.

Cattlemans Rest Motor Inn, cnr Bridge & Plant Streets, ✆4787 3555. 38 units, licensed restaurant (closed Sunday), undercover parking, room service, pool, spa - ✪$69.

Charters Towers Heritage Lodge, 79-97 Flinders Highway, ✆4787 4088 or ✆1800 880 444 (toll free). 17 units, playground, barbecue, undercover parking, room service, pool - ✪$68.

York Street Bed & Breakfast, 58 York Street, ✆4787 1028. 5 rooms, pool - ✪$65.

Main Street, Charters Towers

Country Road, Flinders Highway, ©4787 2422. 18 units, barbecue, undercover parking, pool - ✪$48-56.

Caravan Parks

Dalrymple Tourist Van Park, Lynd Highway, ©4787 1121. 100 sites, barbecue, pool - powered sites ✪$15 for two, cabins $40-55 for two.

Charters Towers Caravan Park, 37 Mt Leyshon Road, ©4787 7944. 50 sites, barbecue, pool - powered sites ✪$14 for two.

Mexican Tourist Park, 75 Church Street, ©4787 1161. 22 sites, pool - powered sites ✪$9 for two, cabins $34-43 for two, on-site vans $34-39 for two.

Eating Out

Two restaurants worth dining at are *Lawsons*, 82- 90 Mosman Street, ©4787 4333, and *Gold City Chinese Restaurant*, 64 Mosman Street, ©4787 7609.

POINTS OF INTEREST

The **Venus Gold Battery**, in Milchester Road, contains a restored gold crushing mill which operated for a century. It is ⊕open from 9am-5pm daily with guided tours available. Admission prices are ✪$3 adults and $1 for children.

The **Zara Clark Museum and Military Display** is at 36 Mosman Street. The aim of the complex is to enshrine the history of Charters Towers, particularly the nostalgia of its gold rush era. There is a range of memorabilia, and some interesting period photographs. It is ⊕open from 10am-3pm daily and costs adults ✪$3 and children $1.

Ravenswood is about 60km east of Charters Towers. It is also a heritage town and another centre of the gold rush. Although it once had no fewer than 55 pubs, it now has a population of less than one hundred. The town seems largely untouched by time.

Burdekin Falls Dam is a large catchment area that now provides the once dry cities of the coast with a plentiful water supply. Nearby, **Burdekin Dam Holiday Park Motel**, ✆4770 3178, offers accommodation and activities for patrons, $45-55 for two.

The Hinterland is to the north, sweeping towards the Gulf. Volcanoes once peppered the area, and the vast underground **Undara Lava Tubes** have become a notable attraction. The trip from Charters Towers to Undara covers a distance of about 380km (238 miles). From Charters Towers, take the Gregory Development Road north to Greenvale, then on to Lynd Junction, then a further 93km (58 miles) along the same road. Turn left onto the Gulf Development Road and travel towards Mt Surprise before taking another left turn at the signposted Undara turn-off. From there it is 15km (9 miles) to the **Undara Lava Lodge**, which has bed & breakfast for ✪$109 per person per night, ✆4097 1411. They offer several different tours of the Undara Experience, starting from ✪$33 adults, $16.50 children for two hours, up to a full day tour for $93 adults, ✆1800 990 992 for reservations.

There is a website at ☞www.undara-experience.com.au, which you can check out beforehand to see if you think the attraction is worth the long drive.

BOWEN

Map J
Population 14,100

LOCATION AND CHARACTERISTICS

Situated just north of the Whitsunday Islands, Bowen is a town where the ocean laps the edges of the main street. It is 210km (130 miles) south of Townsville on the Bruce Highway, and has one of the best climates in Australia. The surrounding coast is indented with innumerable small headlands and quiet coral beaches. Inland, the Don River Plain is a fruit growing region.

HOW TO GET THERE

By Rail

Bowen is accessible by rail, ✆13 2235 for details, schedules and current fares.

By Coach

Greyhound Pioneer, ✆13 2030, and McCaffertys, ✆13 1499 service Bowen.

By Road

On the Bruce Highway, 210km south of Townsville.

VISITOR INFORMATION

The Bowen Visitor Information Centre is on the Bruce Highway, Bowen, ✆4786 4222.

ACCOMMODATION AND SERVICES

There is no shortage of accommodation here.

Castle Motor Lodge, 6 Don Street, ✆4786 1322. 32 units, licensed restaurant, undercover parking, pool, spa - ✪$63.

Whitsunday Sands Resort, Horseshoe Bay Road, ✆4786 3333. 14 units, barbecue, unlicensed restaurant (closed Sunday), playground, kiosk, pool - ✪$55-60.

Skyview Motel Family Units, 49 Horseshoe Bay Road, ✆4786 2232. 14 units, playground, undercover parking, pool - ✪$52-70.

Queens Beach Motor Hotel, 101 Golf Links Road, ✆4785 1555. 50 units, licensed restaurant, pool - ✪$45-62.

Big Mango Tree, Bruce Highway, ✆4786 2499 or ✆4786 2048. 11 units, playground, transfers, pool - ✪$44-50.

Ocean View, Bruce Highway, Gordon Beach, ✆4786 1377. 12 units, barbecue, undercover parking, pool - ✪$44.

Crystal Beach, 38 Horseshoe Bay Road, ✆4786 2561. 4 units, barbecue, pool - ✪$45.

Caravan Parks

Horseshoe Bay Resort, Horseshoe Bay, ✆4786 2564. 40 sites, licensed restaurant, barbecue, kiosk, mini-golf, pool, sauna, spa - powered sites ✪$16 for two, park cabins $32 for two, on-site vans $25 for two.

Bowen Village Caravan & Tourist Park, Bruce Highway (South) ✆4786 1366. 75 sites, barbecue, playground, shop, pool - powered sites ✪$12 for two, cabins $35 for two, on-site vans $20-25 for two.

Rose Bay Caravan Park, Rose Bay, ✆4786 2388. 23 sites, barbecue, pool - powered sites ✪$12 for two, on-site vans $20-25 for two.

Eating Out

If you are interested in dining out, there is the **Peacock Restaurant** at 38 Williams Street, ✆4786 1280, and **Fullagen's Irish Bar & Restaurant** at 37 Herbert Street, ✆4786 1783.

POINTS OF INTEREST

The Bowen Historical Society Museum, 22 Gordon Street, ✆4786 2035. In it you will find shipwreck relics, information on early pioneers and indigenous artefacts. It is ⊕open 10.30am-4pm Mon-Fri and 10.30am-12pm Sunday and costs ✪$2 adults and 50c for children.

Bowen's stunning coastline encapsulates its attraction for visitors. Of particular note are idyllic **Horseshoe Bay** and **Murray Bay**. **Queens Beach** is also a popular haven.

In the southern area of Bowen, swimming, fishing, diving and snorkelling are year-round activities, and for those who prefer to stay on terra firma, there is fossiking for sapphires, amethysts, crystals and opalised woods.

EUNGELLA NATIONAL PARK

Map J

LOCATION AND CHARACTERISTICS

This stunning National Park is 84km (52 miles) inland from Mackay, and the bitumen road leading to it follows the Pioneer River and its tributaries up the valley past Finch Hatton, and through Eungella township at the top of the range. Finch Hatton Gorge has attractive mountain-fed waterfalls, a natural swimming pool, plus good walking tracks.

The Broken River area provides shady pools for swimming, and well marked bush walking tracks are a feature of the Park. If you are lucky you may see a platypus near the bridge.

VISITOR INFORMATION

For information on all National Parks, the organisations to contact for information are the Environmental Protection Agency, ✆3224 5641, or the Queensland National Parks and Wildlife Service, ✆3227 8187 (Naturally Queensland). Connect online to ✇www.env.qld.gov.au

ACCOMMODATION AND SERVICES

Meals and accommodation are available at **Broken River Mountain Retreat**, ✆4958 4528. It has 4 units, guided activities including platypus viewing, a licensed restaurant, playground and pool - ✪$58.

At the top of the range at Eungella, the fully licensed **Historic Eungella Chalet Mountain Lodge**, ✆4958 4509, has 12 rooms, a playground and pool - ✪$45-65.

A permit is required to **camp** in any of the local National Parks, and this can be obtained from the Ranger at Seaforth, ✆4959 0410, the Ranger at Eungella, ✆4958 4552, or from the Queensland National

Parks and Wildlife Service, cnr Wood & River Street, Mackay, ✆4951 8788. Typically, it costs ✪$3.50 per person per night to camp.

CAPE HILLSBOROUGH

Map J

LOCATION AND CHARACTERISTICS

Located 47km (29 miles) north of Mackay, the Cape Hillsborough National Park provides a beachfront picnic area with barbecue facilities. The park is relatively small (830ha - 2050 acres), but it is typical of the best of North Queensland, with rainforests, beaches and abundant wildlife. Walking tracks take you to billabongs, great lookouts and unusual volcanic formations. The fishing in the park is excellent.

HOW TO GET THERE

By Road

To get to the park take the Bruce Highway north from Mackay, then turn right at The Leap.

ACCOMMODATION AND SERVICES

The Cape Hillsborough Holiday Resort, ✆4959 0262, offers 10 units at ✪$59 a double per night, as well as 100 camping sites at $10 for two per night.

There is a licensed restaurant, barbecue area, undercover parking, good facilities and a pool.

Smallys Beach, Cape Hillsborough National Park

Mackay

HALLIDAY BAY

Map J

LOCATION AND CHARACTERISTICS

Situated north of Mackay, near the town of Seaforth, Halliday Bay is noted for its white sandy beach and safe swimming enclosure.

The bay adjoins **McBride's Point National Park**, and has a shop and boat hire facilities. The Bay is named after Captain Halliday, whose century-old stone cottage is still standing.

ACCOMMODATION AND SERVICES

Halliday Bay Units, in Headland Drive, ✆4959 0322, have 54 units, a licensed restaurant, playground, tennis court, kiosk, sailing and a swimming pool - ✪$65. There are also 18 Holiday Units at $55 per night.

PROSERPINE

Map F
Population 2800

LOCATION AND CHARACTERISTICS

Proserpine, 127km (80 miles) north of Mackay, is mainly a sugar cane town. It serves as the centre of the Whitsunday region, in administrative terms, but most visitors by-pass its scenic charm on their way to the more seductive coastline. The town has full facilities and a good range of accommodation.

You may wish to stay close to the Bruce Highway on a northward/southward journey, but if you plan to be in the Whitsundays area for any significant length of time, and are not planning to stay on an island resort, the coastal settlements of Airlie Beach and Shute Harbour have all the good views.

West of the town is Lake Proserpine, where waterskiing is a popular sport.

HOW TO GET THERE

By Air

Ansett, ✆13 1300, and Sunstate, ✆13 1313, have frequent flights to Prosperine.

By Rail

The Sunlander departs Brisbane for Proserpine every Tuesday, Thursday and Saturday, and departs Cairns on the return journey every Monday, Thursday and Saturday, ✆13 2235.

By Coach

Both McCaffertys, ✆13 1499, and Greyhound Pioneer, ✆13 2030, stop at Proserpine.

By Road

Proserpine, on the Bruce Highway 127km (80 miles) north of Mackay, is the nearest major centre. Shute Harbour is a further 30km from there, and 8km from Airlie Beach.

VISITOR INFORMATION

The Whitsunday Information Centre on the Bruce Highway is in Proserpine, ✆4945 3711.

ACCOMMODATION AND SERVICES

Laguna Quays, Kunapipi Springs Road, Repulse Bay, ✆4747 7777 or ✆1800 812 626 (toll free), is not strictly in Proserpine itself, but deserves a mention. It is on the coast 26km south of the town. There are 36 rooms, with 24 suites, 2 licensed restaurants, a playground, room service, bushwalking tracks, watersports, golf, tennis, a pool and sauna - from ✪$250.

Proserpine Motor Lodge, 184 Main Street, ✆4945 1788. 33 units, licensed restaurant, undercover parking, room service, pool - ✪$59.

Whitsunday Palms, Bruce Highway, ✆4945 1868. 6 units, barbecue, undercover parking - ✪$40-42.

Reef Gardens Motel, Bruce Highway, ✆4945 1288. 12 units, barbecue, playground, undercover parking - ✪$38-44.

Anchor Motel Whitsunday, Bruce Highway, ✆4945 1200. 12 units, unlicensed restaurant, undercover parking - ✪$35-37.

Caravan Park
Golden Cane Caravan Park, ✆4945 1540. 25 sites, barbecue, playground, kiosk, pool - powered sites ✪$12 for two, units $28 for two, cabins $38 for two.

Eating Out
Two places to dine at in Proserpine are *Proserpine Village Chinese Restaurant*, 13 Mill Street, ✆4945 2589 and *Pioneer Bistro*, 140 Main Street, ✆4945 3637.

Local Transport
Whitsunday Transit buses service the area, ✆4952 2377 for schedule details.

SHUTE HARBOUR

Map F

LOCATION AND CHARACTERISTICS
Shute Harbour is the focal point for departure of many tourist vessels cruising to the Whitsunday Islands. Not only is it the second busiest passenger port in Australia, it boasts the second largest bareboat industry in the world (a bareboat is a boat hired without a crew).

HOW TO GET THERE
By Air
Ansett, ✆13 1300, and Sunstate, ✆13 1313, have frequent flights to nearby Prosperine.

By Rail
The Sunlander departs Brisbane for Proserpine every Tuesday, Thursday and Saturday, and departs Cairns on the return journey every Monday, Thursday and Saturday, ✆13 2235.

Mackay

Boats moored in Shute Harbour

By Coach

Both McCaffertys, ☎13 1499, and Greyhound Pioneer, ☎13 2030, stop at nearby Proserpine.

By Road

Off the Bruce Highway 127km (80 miles) north of Mackay.

VISITOR INFORMATION

Use the contact details for Whitsunday Tourism, listed under *Visitor Information* for Whitsunday Islands, or visit the Tourist Information Centre at Airlie Beach, 277 Shute Harbour Road, ☎4946 6665.

ACCOMMODATION AND SERVICES

Shute Harbour is mostly a gateway for cruises out to the islands, and is one of the smaller satellite areas for Proserpine, as well as being superceded by Airlie Beach as an accommodation centre. Nevertheless, there are a couple of places to stay here.

Coral Point Lodge, Harbour Avenue, ☎4946 9500 or ☎1800 077 611. 10 units, views take in Shute Harbour and the Whitsunday Islands, unlicensed restaurant, undercover parking, transfers, pool - ✪$70-82.

Shute Harbour, Shute Harbour Road, ☎4946 9131. 12 units, licensed restaurant, car parking, room service, pool - ✪$50-70.

Caravan Park

Flame Tree Tourist Village, Shute Harbour Road, ✆4946 9388 or ✆1800 069 388. 100 sites, barbecue, playground, shop, heated pool - powered sites ✪$17 for two, villas $55-60 for two, units $50-55 for two, cabins $40-45 for two, on-site vans $30-35 for two.

Eating Out

For decent meals at reasonable prices, try *The Catalina Bistro Bar* on Shute Harbour Road, ✆4946 9797.

AIRLIE BEACH

Map F

LOCATION AND CHARACTERISTICS

Airlie Beach, the main resort town on the Whitsunday coast, has a relaxed atmosphere, and is 8km (5 miles) from Shute Harbour, 24km (15 miles) from Proserpine.

The town borders the 20,000ha Conway National Park, and is the mainland centre for the Whitsundays.

Airlie Beach is a picturesque village and offers a lot to the holiday-maker on its own account, but when you add the close proximity of the Reef islands, it is not hard to figure out why some people choose to stay at Airlie and take day trips to the islands.

HOW TO GET THERE

By Air

Ansett, ✆13 1300, and Sunstate, ✆13 1313, have frequent flights to Proserpine.

By Rail

The Sunlander departs Brisbane for Proserpine every Tuesday, Thursday and Saturday, and departs Cairns on the return journey every Monday, Thursday and Saturday, ✆13 2235.

By Coach

Both McCaffertys, ✆13 1499, and Greyhound Pioneer, ✆13 2030, stop at Airlie Beach.

Mackay

By Road

Proserpine, on the Bruce Highway 127km (80 miles) north of Mackay, is the nearest major centre. From there it is 24km (15 miles) to Airlie Beach.

VISITOR INFORMATION

The Airlie Tourist Information Centre is at 277 Shute Harbour Road, Airlie Beach, ✆4946 6665, and can be emailed at:

✉ abtic@whitsunday.net.au

ACCOMMODATION AND SERVICES

This is the major costal mainland accommodation centre for the Whitsundays. The area code is (07).

Whitsunday Vista Quest Resort, 1 Hermitage Drive, ✆4946 7007. 10 units, barbecue, undercover parking, pool, spa - ✪$149-328.

Mediterranean Resorts, Golden Orchid Drive, ✆4946 6391. 12 units, undercover parking, spa, 2 pools - ✪$65-109.

Coral Sea Resort, 25 Ocean View Avenue, ✆4946 6458 or ✆1800 075 061 (toll free). 25 units, two licensed restaurants, room service, pool - ✪$130-200.

Airlie Beach Motor Lodge, Lamond Street, ✆4946 6418 or ✆1800 810 925 (toll free). 4 units, barbecue, undercover parking, pool, sauna - ✪$82-92.

Colonial Palms Motor Inn, cnr Shute Harbour Road & Hermitage Drive, ✆4946 7166 or ✆1800 075 114 (toll free). 30 units, licensed restaurant, undercover parking, room service, pool, spa - ✪$80-90.

Whitsunday Wanderers Resort, Shute Harbour Road, ✆4946 6446 or ✆1800 075 069. 104 units, licensed restaurant, barbecue, playground, table tennis, gymnasium, mini golf, volleyball, pool, 2 spas - ✪$65-109.

Airlie Beach Hotel/Motel, 16 The Esplanade, Airlie Beach, ✆4946 6233. 30 units, pool - ✪$55-90. Every Tuesday and Thursday from 7.30pm the famous Charity Toad Races are held here. All proceeds are given to worthy causes, but you can win cruises and prizes at these family-fun nights.

The Islands Inn, Shute Harbour Road, ✆4946 6755 or ✆4946 6943. 32 units, barbecue, licensed restaurant, pool, spa - ✪$55-65.

Airlie Court Holiday Units, 382 Shute Harbour Road, ✆4946 6218. 6 units, licensed restaurant, undercover parking - ✪$50-85.

Airlie Island Traders, Shute Harbour Road, ✆4946 4056. 9 units, barbecue, playground, undercover parking, heated pool - ✪$45-75.

Caravan Parks

Airlie Cove Resort Van Park, cnr Shute Harbour & Ferntree Roads, ✆4946 6727. (No dogs allowed) 64 sites, barbecue, playground, tennis, pool, spa - powered sites ✪$18 for two, cabins $35-85 for two.

Island Getaway Holidays Resort, cnr Shute Harbour & Jubilee Pocket Roads, ✆4946 6228. 154 sites, barbecue, playground, shop, tennis and mini golf, pool, spa - powered sites ✪$17 for two, units $94 for two, cabins $39 for two.

Shute Harbour Gardens Caravan Park, Shute Harbour Road, ✆4946 6483. 40 sites, barbecue, kiosk, pool - powered sites ✪$15 for two, villas $60 for two, cabins $50 for two.

There is a **Youth Hostel** at 394 Shute Harbour Road, ✆4946 6312 or ✆1800 247 251. It has 17 rooms at ✪$19 per person twin share.

Local Transport

If you require local transport, the Whitsunday Taxi Service can be contacted on ✆1800 811 388.

POINTS OF INTEREST

The Barefoot Bushman's Wildlife Park, Lot 2, Shute Harbour Road, Cannonvale, ✆4946 1480, has a terrific array of Australian wildlife with shows throughout the day. There are pythons, brown snakes, lizards, frogs, ducks, pelicans, owls, kookaburras, possums, wombats, fruit bats, native birds, doves, emus, dingoes and crocodiles, to name a few. Highlights include the Snake Show, where the world's deadliest snakes are put on display, and the Crocodile Feeding, where you can see these huge reptiles snapping up their lunch. The Wildlife Park is

Mackay

⊙open 9am-4pm every day and admission is ✪$15 adults, $7 children and $40 for families.

ACTIVITIES

Whitsunday Parasail, 25 Ocean View Avenue, Airlie Beach, ℭ4948 0000 - single flight ✪$40, tandem flight $80.

Brandy Creek Trail Rides, Lot 15 Brandy Creek Road, Cannon Valley, ℭ4946 6665 or ℭ4946 1121 - half-day escorted trail rides, departing daily 9am and 2.30pm - includes courtesy coach, billy tea and damper - proper clothing is supplied and horses are available to suit all riding expertise levels - ✪$41 adults and $35 children.

CHARTER FLIGHTS

Air Whitsunday Seaplanes, Air Whitsunday Drive, Airlie Beach, ℭ4946 9111, offer:

Panorama - two hours of snorkelling in lagoons only accessible by seaplane - a stop at Whitehaven Beach - champagne picnic at extra charge ($20) - 4 hours duration - ✪$249 adults, $130 children.

Reef Explorer - fly over all the Whitsunday Islands - land at Whitehaven Beach for two hours - 3 hours duration - ✪$169 adults, $115 children.

Reef Adventure - panoramic views of the Whitsunday Islands - land on the reef and board a coral viewing sub - snorkelling with tuition - 3 hours duration - ✪$199 adults, $130 children.

Hayman Day Trip - flight to Hayman Island - full use of resort facilities - return flight departs 4.30pm - 7 hours duration - ✪$129 adults, $95 children.

CRUISES

There are countless companies operating cruise and sailing vessels through this coral paradise, and the Visitor Information Centre has more material than you will probably have time to read through. The choices are overwhelming, and may come down to the brochure with the brightest pictures!

The following details will give you a basis for comparison.

Fantasea Cruises, 11 Shute Harbour Road, Airlie Beach, ✆4946 5811 or ✆4946 5111 (bookings), offer:

Great Barrier Reef Day Cruise to Reefworld - semi-sub coral viewing, snorkelling equipment including hygienic mouthpiece, buffet lunch, morning and afternoon teas, fresh water showers and large sundeck area, courtesy pick-up from accommodation, large underwater viewing chamber - ✪$135 adults, $120 children (4-14), $316 for families - daily 8.15am-5.20pm from Shute Harbour.

Three Island Adventure - visit Whitehaven Beach, Hamilton and Daydream Islands - beach games at Whitehaven and pool facilities at Daydream, morning and afternoon tea, courtesy pick-up - ✪$75 adults, $37 children (4-14), $187 for families - departs Shute Harbour 8.45am, returns 5.20pm.

Hamilton Island Day Cruise - ✪$45 adults, $22.50 children - daily from Shute Harbour 8.15am, 9.15am, 10.15am or 11.15am.

Whitehaven Beach & Hamilton Island - ✪$59 adults, $29 children, $147 for families - departs Shute Harbour 8.45am.

Island Discovery Pass - one day pass for travel between Daydream, South Molle and Hamilton islands - ✪$45 adults, $22.50 children, $112.50 for families - departs Shute Harbour 8.45am.

Whale Watching Day Cruise - these are usually held July-September, depending upon the arrival and departure of these fascinating creatures - ✆4946 5811 for seasonal prices and departure times.

Reefsleep - 2 days' and 1 night's accommodation at the Reefworld facility - snorkelling and scuba diving - underwater viewing - all meals - from ✪$298.

Fantasea has a website at ☞www.fantasea.com.au

Seatrek Whitsunday Cruises, Shop 1, 283 Shute Harbour Road, Airlie Beach, ✆4946 4366 or ✆4946 5255, offer:

South Molle Island Day Trip - includes windsurfing, catamarans, paddle skis, golf - daily ✪$29 adults, $25 children, $75 for families - departs Shute Harbour - 9am-5pm.

Whitsunday All Over Cruises, 398 Shute Harbour Road, ℂ4946 6900 or ℂ1300 366 494 (bookings), offer:

3 Islands in 3 Days - launch transfer between Daydream, South Molle and Long Islands over a 3 day period - ✪$45 adults, $25 children.

Club Crocodile Long Island Adventure Pack - transfers from Shute Harbour to Long Island - lunch included - use of facilities at Club Crocodile - island exploration - ✪$35 adults, $15 children, $85 for families.

South Molle Island Day Trip - transfer to South Molle Island - lunch included - use of facilities - ✪$35 adults, $15 children, $85 for families.

Yellow Sub Cruise - includes courtesy coach, morning tea, picnic lunch, snorkelling gear, talk by marine biologist, guided island tours, guided coral viewing in an air-conditioned semi-submersible, visit to Daydream Island Beach Club for approximately an hour before returning to the mainland - ✪$67 adult, $35 child - $175 family - daily - departs Shute Harbour at 9.15am, South Molle at 9.30am - returns 5pm.

Mantaray Charters, 28 Jones Road, Cannonvale, ℂ4946 4579 or ℂ4946 6665 (bookings) - full day cruise taking in Whitehaven Bay and Mantaray Beach - diving and snorkelling - some equipment provided - ✪$55 adults, $28 children, $150 for families, tropical lunch an extra $8 adults and $5 children - departs Abel Point 9am.

DIVING

Whitsunday Dive Charters, 5 Airlie Crescent, Airlie Beach, ℂ4946 5366 - a fast dive vessel takes you out to Bait Reef for the day - departs Abel Point Marina 8.45am - from ✪$165 diving and $115 snorkelling.

Reef Dive Whitsundays, Shute Harbour Road, Airlie Beach, ℂ4946 6508 or 1800 075 120 (free call) - live-aboard trip over 3 nights, with all meals and 10 dives (including 2 night dives) - ✪$440 per person.

Oceania Dive, 257 Shute Harbour Road, Airlie Beach, ©1800 075 035 (enquiries) or ©4946 6032 (bookings) - PADI open water courses - cruise to the edge of the Coral Sea, through the Whitsunday Islands - dive the Elizabeth and Stucco Reefs - from ✪$300 for a 4 day open water course - advanced courses, 3 days and 3 nights for $515.

THE WHITSUNDAYS

Map F

LOCATION AND CHARACTERISTICS

The Whitsundays consist of 74 islands from the Cumberland and Northumberland Island groups, and they form the largest offshore island chain on Australia's east coast.

The islands are the remains of a mountain range that was drowned when sea levels rose at the end of the last ice age. Most of them have National Park status, and all are situated in the marine park.

The islands were named by Captain Cook when he sailed through the passage on Whitsunday, 1770. Some like to point out that it was not actually Whitsunday, since the good old captain neglected to take into account the fact that he had crossed the international date line, and so was a day out. However, because he made so few nautical and mathematical errors on his journey, Captain Cook is usually forgiven his Whitsunday oversight.

Later, when European settlement began on several of the islands, there were some violent confrontations with the resident Aborigines which tarnish the history of this idyllic place.

CLIMATE

This is a tropical, sub-rainforest region. Daytime temperatures April-October are 20 to 24C, night are 14 to 18C. During November-March, the "green season", daytime are 24 to 30C, and night are 18 to 26C. The water temperature remains 20 to 22C throughout the year.

Mackay

VISITOR INFORMATION

The Whitsunday Visitors and Convention Bureau, ✆4946 6673, is found on the corner of Shute Harbour and Mandalay Roads, one kilometre from Airlie. They can be emailed at:
✎tw@whitsundayinformation.com.au and have a web page at 👁www.whitsundayinformation.com.au

Alternatively, there is a website at 👁www.whitsunday.net.au

The Whitsunday Information Centre is on the Bruce Highway in Proserpine, ✆4945 3711.

CAMPING

There are basic camping facilities on Hook, North Molle, Whitsunday, Henning, Border, Haslewood, Shaw, Thomas and Repulse Islands. These consist of toilets and picnic tables, with a ranger patrolling. Costs are ✪$3.50 per person per night. All permits can be obtained over the phone by calling the Naturally Queensland Information Centre in Brisbane on ✆3227 8197 or emailing them at:
✎nqic@env.qld.gov.au

For more information on camping in the region, contact any QNP&WS branch.

WHITSUNDAY ISLAND

Although Whitsunday is the largest of the island in the Whitsunday Group, it does not have a resort. But it does have Whitehaven Beach, the longest and best beach in the whole group, and the destination of many cruises. There is good snorkelling off the southern end of the beach.

There are several camping sites on the island, and more information can be obtained from Naturally Queensland, listed under *Camping* above.

WHITSUNDAY GROUP

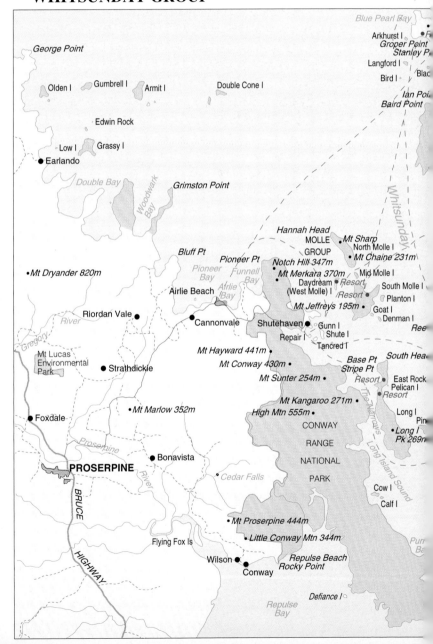

Blue Pearl Bay
Arkhurst I
Groper Point
Stanley P
Langford I
Bird I
Blac
Ian Poi
Baird Point

George Point

Olden I
Gumbrell I
Armit I
Double Cone I

Edwin Rock

Low I
Grassy I
Earlando

Double Bay
Grimston Point
Woodwark Bay
Whitsunday

Hannah Head
MOLLE
GROUP
Mt Sharp
North Molle I
Mt Chaine 231m

Bluff Pt
Pioneer Pt
Notch Hill 347m
Mt Merkara 370m
Mid Molle I
Pioneer Bay
Funnell Bay
Daydream
(West Molle) I
Resort
South Molle I

• Mt Dryander 820m
Airlie Beach
Airlie Bay
Mt Jeffreys 195m
Resort
Planton I
Goat I
Denman I

Riordan Vale •
Cannonvale •
Shutehaven •
Gunn I
Shute I
Ree

Repair I
Tancred I

River
Mt Hayward 441m •
Base Pt
Stripe Pt
South Hea

Gregory
Mt Lucas
Environmental
Park
• Strathdickie
Mt Conway 430m •
Mt Sunter 254m •
Resort
East Rock
Pelican I
Resort

• Mt Marlow 352m
Mt Kangaroo 271m •
High Mtn 555m •
CONWAY
Long I
Pin

Foxdale •
RANGE
Long I
Pk 269m

Prosperine
Bonavista •
NATIONAL
PARK
Long Island Sound

PROSERPINE
River
Cedar Falls
Cow I

BRUCE
Calf I

• Mt Proserpine 444m
• Little Conway Mtn 344m

HIGHWAY
Flying Fox Is
Wilson •
Repulse Beach
Rocky Point
Purr
Ba

Conway

Defiance I

Repulse Bay

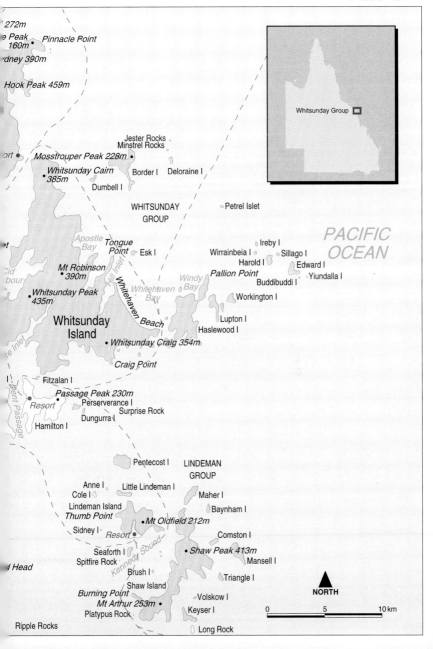

272m
Peak 160m • Pinnacle Point
dney 390m

Hook Peak 459m

Whitsunday Group

Jester Rocks
Minstrel Rocks
ort • Mosstrouper Peak 228m •
Whitsunday Cairn • 385m   Border I   Deloraine I
Dumbell I

WHITSUNDAY
GROUP   ○ Petrel Islet

PACIFIC
OCEAN

Apostle
Bay   Tongue
t   Point   Esk I
                                    ○ Ireby I
                        Wirrainbeia I ○   ○ Sillago I
Cid   Harold I   Edward I
bour   Mt Robinson   Pallion Point   Yiundalla I
        • 390m   Buddibuddi I
Windy
• Whitsunday Peak   Whitehaven Bay
435m   Bay
                                    Workington I
        Whitsunday   Beach
        Island   Lupton I
                        • Whitsunday Craig 354m   Haslewood I

e Inlet
                Craig Point

I   Fitzalan I
ent Passage
        Passage Peak 230m
        Perserverance I
Resort   Surprise Rock
        Dungurra I
Hamilton I

                Pentecost I   LINDEMAN
                        GROUP
        Anne I   Little Lindeman I
        Cole I ○   Maher I
        Lindeman Island   Baynham I
        Thumb Point
                • Mt Oldfield 212m
        Sidney I   Resort •
                                Comston I
        Seaforth I   • Shaw Peak 413m
        Spitfire Rock   Mansell I
                Brush I ○
        Burning Point   Shaw Island   Triangle I
        Mt Arthur 253m •   ○ Volskow I
I Head   Platypus Rock   Keyser I

Ripple Rocks   ○ Long Rock

NORTH

0   5   10 km

MACKAY

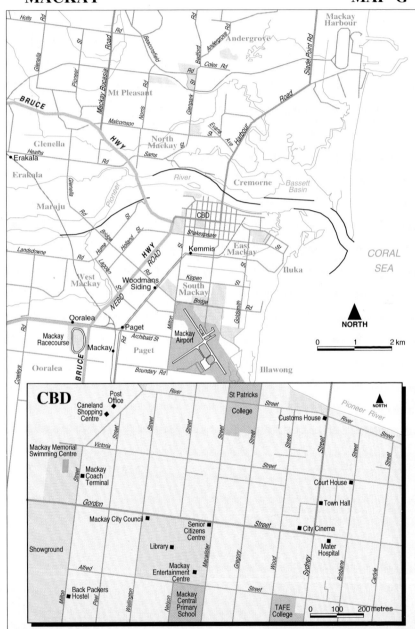

LINDEMAN ISLAND

Map F

LOCATION AND CHARACTERISTICS

The island has 20km (12 miles) of walking tracks that lead through 500ha (1235 acres) of National Park. There are seven secluded beaches, and at dusk from the top of Mt Oldfield, you can see the sun set over islands that stretch to the horizon in every direction.

Lindeman has an area of 8 sq km, most of which is national park, and was named after George Lindeman, whose job in the Royal Navy was to chart safe passages through the Whitsunday Islands.

The first resort was opened by Angus and Elizabeth Nicholson in 1923, and it stayed in their family until it was sold in 1979.

Lindeman has six beaches and 20km of walking trails. Its highest point is Mt Oldfield, 210m. There is a resident Park Ranger who will advise and even accompany walkers.

HOW TO GET THERE

By Air

Access is by air from Mackay or Shute Harbour, and can be included in room package rates on request.

By Sea

For a water taxi from Hamilton Island, ℭ4946 9633 to make arrangements through the resort. Roylen Cruises, ℭ4955 3066, have a launch service from Mackay.

VISITOR INFORMATION

Contact the resort directly or follow the links to Lindeman Island at the Club Med website: ☜www.clubmed.com.au

ACCOMMODATION AND SERVICES

Accommodation is available at **Club Med Lindeman Island**, ℭ4946 9633, which opened its doors on Lindeman Island in 1992, and by 1994 had won the Hotel/Resort of the Year award.

Mackay

Resort facilities are: boutique, restaurants, laundry, sports club-house, medical facilities, nightclub, recorded classical music concerts, card room, picnics, golf course (9-holes), tennis, aerobics, volleyball, basketball, archery, table tennis, football, cricket, badminton, hiking in the National Park, sailing, windsurfing, paddle skis, snorkelling, 2 swimming pools, seaboat trips, beach towels, Kids' Club.

Room facilities are: air-conditioning, private bathroom, balcony patio, TV, phone, bar fridge, tea/coffee making facilities, overhead ceiling fan.

Tariffs for one night per person/twin share (including light plane transfers from Mackay) are ✪$235 adults, $205 children 12-14; $120 children 4-11.

The above rates include all meals plus meal time drinks (beer, wine and juices). Cheaper packages include transfers from the Whitsundays. Enquire also about complete holiday packages, which include return air fares.

Not included in the tariffs are: the scuba diving course on the Great Barrier Reef, special excursions, and drinks at the bar.

Reservations can be made online at the Club Med website, or direct through the Resort, ✆4946 9333.

Credit cards accepted: American Express, Visa, Diners Club, MasterCard and Bankcard.

POINTS OF INTEREST

DIVING

There is not much here for scuba divers, but the Resort arranges diving trips out to the Reef. Snorkelling trips to Hardy Lagoon take place several days a week.

SOUTH MOLLE ISLAND

Map F

LOCATION AND CHARACTERISTICS

The island covers 405ha (1000 acres) and is 4km long and 2.4km wide. It is situated in the heart of Whitsunday Passage, and offers fishing, golf, tennis, water skiing, coral viewing, scuba diving, parasailing and bushwalking.

South Molle has an area of 4 sq km, and is the largest of the Molle group. It is close to Mid Molle, and in fact you can walk from South Molle to Mid Molle at any time. Another island that is very close is Daydream.

The oldest of the resorts in the Whitsunday Group, South Molle is mostly national park and offers some good, if short, walks. The highest point is Mt Jeffreys (198m), and from it there are great views of the surrounding islands. Balancing Rock and Spion Kop also allow you to take in breathtaking vistas.

The first European settler was Henry George Lamond, who moved in with his wife and children in 1927 and stayed for ten years. There is a memorial to his son, Hal, on top of Lamond Hill.

South Molle is very much a family resort, there is even a pre-school nursery as well as activities for school-age children.

HOW TO GET THERE

By Air

Ansett, ©13 1300, fly to South Molle.

By Sea

Access is by launch departing daily from Shute Harbour, Blue Ferries (Fantasea), ©4946 5111. A return fare is ©$16.

VISITOR INFORMATION

The resort can be contacted on ©4946 9433. The web site is ©www.southmolleisland.com.au with an email service at: ✉info@southmolleisland.com.au

ACCOMMODATION AND SERVICES

Accommodation is available at **South Molle Island Resort**, ©4946 9433. 44 units, licensed restaurant, swimming pool, spa, sauna, tennis, squash, golf - full board ✪$310-390 a double per day.

The Resort has five different room categories, none of which are the most modern available in the Whitsundays, though they are definitely comfortable:

The Family rooms overlook the golf course and National Park, and have a double bedroom that can be shut off from the rest of the unit. These are ideal for a family of six.

Golf rooms also overlook the golf course and can accommodate a maximum of two.

Beachcomber units are freestanding and are located on the beachfront, with unobstructed ocean views. They can accommodate a maximum of four.

Reef units are set back 30-40 metres from the beach in a garden setting, and are handy to all facilities. They can accommodate four.

Whitsunday units have prime beachfront locations, facing the Whitsunday passage. Ground floor rooms have patios and those on the first floor have balconies. They can accommodate a maximum of four.

Resort facilities are: golf course, swimming pool, wading pool, kids' club, spa, sauna, beach towels, hairdresser, gift shop, coffee shop, live entertainment, disco, tennis, squash, volleyball, archery, gymnasium, snorkelling, scuba diving (tuition available), parasailing, water skiing, paddle skis, organised beach sports, windsurfers, catamarans, Great Barrier Reef cruises, day cruises to other islands and EFTPOS.

Room facilities are: private bathroom, ceiling fan, colour TV, refrigerator, IDD/STD phone, radio, tea/coffee making facilities, iron, ironing board and rooms serviced daily.

Tariffs for 2 adults and 2 children (minimum) are:

Family rooms - ✪$450 full board, $330 room only.

Tariffs for one night per person/twin share are:

Golf rooms - ✪$155 full board, $110 room only.

Beachcomber units -   ✪$215 full board, $170 room only.

Reef units -   ✪$175 full board, $135 room only.

Whitsunday units -   ✪$195 full board, $150 room only.

The above rates include all meals. They do not include golf balls, tennis balls, squash balls or fuel powered watersports.

Reservations can be made through the resort, ✆4946 9433, or on the website. All major credit cards accepted.

POINTS OF INTEREST

DIVING

There is a Resort Dive Shop that offers short courses for beginners, and organises trips out to various parts of the reef. Contact the Resort for more information.

LONG ISLAND

Map F

LOCATION AND CHARACTERISTICS

The island is directly off the coast of Shute Harbour, and adjoins the Whitsunday Passage. It is deliberately underdeveloped, and the untamed tropical rainforest and protected Palm Bay Lagoon make for a very informal holiday.

There are 13km (8 miles) of well graded bushwalking tracks, and a variety of beaches for swimming and fishing.

Long Island is separated from the mainland by a channel that is only 500m wide, making it the closest resort island to the Queensland coast. It has an area of 12 sq km, but is about 11km long, so it is apparent that it is extremely narrow, only about 1.5km at its widest.

The island was originally called Port Molle, named after the Lieutenant Governor of the colony of NSW from 1814, who had his name liberally sprinkled on islands in the area. We still have North, Mid and South Molle, but there was also West Molle, which became Daydream, and this one whose name was changed to Long by Matthew Flinders.

Mackay

The first resorts opened in the 1930s; one at Happy Bay, the other at Palm Bay. The Happy Bay establishment lasted up to 1983 when new buyers changed the name to Whitsunday 100 and tried to make it into another Great Keppel, but without much success. It was taken over and refurbished by Contiki in 1986 for their 18 to 35 clientele, then in 1990 new owners thought the name "The Island" would catch on, but in 1991 it became the Radisson Long Island Resort, and in January 1994, Club Crocodile.

Palm Bay Resort, in the southern part of the island, was devastated by a cyclone in the mid-1970s, but is back in operation as the Palm Bay Hideaway a low-key, old fashioned resort without all the commercial razzle-dazzle.

There was another resort at Paradise Bay, on the southern tip of Long Island, but it has never seemed to have the appeal of the others and has opened and closed several times.

Long Island has 20km of bush walks through the National Park, and there are some nice sandy beaches on its western side, but at Happy Valley the tidal variations cause the water to be so far from the beach that it is easier to swim in the pool. The box jellyfish makes its appearance in the vicinity from March to November. The beaches on the eastern side tend to be rocky and usually windy, but the dredging that has been undertaken at Palm Bay makes it ideal for swimming, and for mooring yachts.

HOW TO GET THERE

By Air
Ansett, ©13 1300, fly to Long Island.

By Sea
Access is daily by launch from Shute Harbour, and arrangements can be made through your selected accommodation.

VISITOR INFORMATION

The Club Crocodile Resort can be contacted on ✆4946 9233, and for a preliminary look at what the island has to offer, follow the links to Long Island at ☞www.clubcrocodile.com.au

ACCOMMODATION AND SERVICES

There are two choices on Long Island:

Club Crocodile Long Island, ✆4946 9400 (a sister to the Club Crocodile at Airlie Beach, Shute Harbour Road, ✆4946 7155), has 54 garden rooms (3-star), 86 beachfront units (3-star) and 16 lodge rooms (2-star).

Resort facilities are: restaurants, cafe, barbecue, two bars, two swimming pools, spa, sauna, tennis courts, dance club and bar, extensive range of watersports, gymnasium, paddleboards, catamaran, coral viewing, resort store, games room, Kids' Club, laundry/ironing facilities and EFTPOS.

Room facilities are: private bathroom, air-conditioning (Beachfront), refrigerator, tea/coffee making facilities, radio, colour TV, balcony, ceiling fans, IDD/STD telephone and daily cleaning service.

Tariffs for a double room per night, full board, are:

Garden - ✪$310
Beachfront - ✪$350
Lodge - ✪$194

Child rates, 3-17 years, ✪$45 per night.

Not included in the above rates are scuba diving, water taxi, fuel powered water sports or diving.

Contact the resort for reservations or book online. Credit cards accepted: American Express, Bankcard, Visa, MasterCard, Diners Club.

Palm Bay Hideaway accommodation consists of cabins and bures.

Resort facilities are: catamarans, windsurfing, volleyball, snorkelling gear, paddle skis, bar, dining room, hand line fishing gear, barbecue, swimming pool, spa, laundry/ironing facilities, lounge area, general store, outdoor dining terrace, tree house, open fireplace.

Room facilities are: private bathrooms, verandah, tea/coffee making facilities, ceiling fans, refrigerator, cooking facilities and utensils.

Tariffs for a double room per night are:

Cabin - ✪$224.

Unit - ✪$284.

Not included in the above rates are water taxi transfers or fuel powered water sports. Credit cards accepted: Visa, MasterCard, Bankcard, American Express.

The resort shop has food supplies for those wishing to utilise the kitchen facilities, but it will obviously be much cheaper to take your own provisions.

POINTS OF INTEREST

DIVING

Club Crocodile has a dive shop and can arrange trips out to the Reef.

HAYMAN ISLAND

Map F

LOCATION AND CHARACTERISTICS

The island is a resort offering a balance between luxury living and natural beauty. Curving around the sandy shoreline of the blue lagoon on the south-western side of the island, Hayman looks out toward Langford Reef and an island called Bali Hai. All sports, both on land and water, are catered for at the resort.

Hayman Island has an area of 4 sq km, and is the most northerly of the Whitsunday resort islands. Its resort is one of the most luxurious on the Great Barrier Reef, and in fact is widely considered to be one of the top ten resorts in the world.

In 1866 the island was named after Thomas Hayman, navigator of the HMS *Salamander* which served in these waters for many years. In 1904 the island was leased by Thomas Abel for grazing his cattle, but he sold out in 1907. The first resort was established in 1935 by Bert Hallam and his brother, but this was a simple affair for fishing trips.

Mackay

Reginald Ansett took over the island in 1947, and the fishing resort closed its doors in 1948, then in 1950 the Hayman Resort opened and remained so until 1985 when it was closed for a multi-million dollar rebuild.

There are several bushwalks on Hayman, including an 8km circuit and walks to Blue Pearl Bay or Dolphin Point. It is also possible to walk to nearby Arkhurst Island at low tide.

HOW TO GET THERE

By Air

Ansett Australia, ✆13 1300, flies to Hayman Island.

VISITOR INFORMATION

Contact the resort or go to 👁www.hayman.com.au

ACCOMMODATION AND SERVICES

Hayman Island Resort, ✆4946 1234, offers luxury of the highest quality. Antiques and treasures from around the world, as well as Australian works of art, can be found throughout the resort.

There are three main room categories - Rooms, Suites and Penthouses - with no less than 17 sub-categories, including Palm Garden, Beachfront, Contemporary, Californian, Japanese, Deco, Italian Palazzo, Moroccan and French.

Resort facilities are: six restaurants, cocktail bars, entertainment, pool bar, saltwater swimming pool, two freshwater pools, fully equipped health club, beauty salon, hairdresser, snorkelling, hobie cat sailing, windsurfing, beach volleyball, paddle skis, full and half court tennis, golf target range, lawn croquet, walking tracks, putting green, outdoor jacuzzi/spa, billiards room, table tennis, card and games room, badminton, new release movies on big screen, parasailing, water-skiing, water sleigh, yacht charter, Reef trips, dinghy hire, snorkelling excursions icnics, tennis coaching, game/bottom and reef fishing trips and EFTPOS.

Rooms facilities are: air conditioning, ceiling fan, colour TV, video, IDD/STD telephone, hairdryer, mini bar, bathrobes, room safe, and rooms serviced daily.

Mackay

Typical island in the Whitsunday Group

Tariffs for a double room per night are:

Palm Garden View Rooms -	✪$490
West Wing Rooms -	✪$690
East Wing Rooms -	✪$750
Beachfront Rooms -	✪$750
West Wing Suites -	✪$1,300
East Wing Suites -	✪$1,500.
Contemporary Penthouse -	✪$1,700
Deco Penthouse -	✪$1,800
Italian Palazzo -	✪$2,000
English (2 bedroom) -	✪$2,700
French (3 bedroom) -	✪$3,300

The above rates include breakfast only, and the rest of the meals don't come cheaply either. The wine list is extensive but expensive.

Mackay

Activities not included in the rates are: parasailing, water skiing, water sleigh, yacht charter, Reef trips, dinghy hire, snorkelling excursions picnics, tennis coaching, game/bottom and reef fishing trips.

Reservations can be made through the website, or with the resort, ©4946 1234. All major credit cards are accepted.

POINTS OF INTEREST

DIVING

Hayman is closer to the outer Reef than other resort islands, and Hayman has a full-time dive boat to cater to every diver's desires. Thirty kilometres north-east of Hayman are the Hardy and Black Reefs.

HAMILTON ISLAND

Map F

LOCATION AND CHARACTERISTICS

Hamilton has an area of 6 sq km, and is home to the largest resort in the South Pacific with its own jet airport.

The resort was the brain-child of Gold Coast entrepreneur Keith Williams, with help from friends such as Ansett Airlines. He had originally leased the island for deer farming, but converted this lease to one for tourism.

The workmen moved onto the island in 1982; parts of the complex were operational by 1984; and the entire resort was completed before the end of 1986. All this without interference from the Green Movement, even when the 15-storey condos went up and the airport runways were laid.

In the beginning it was a huge success, but disaster struck in ways that the management could neither foresee or control - firstly the domestic pilots' strike, then the international recession. Finally, in May 1992, Hamilton Island was placed in receivership, but in late 1993 it was successfully floated on the Australian Stock Exchange, and in March 1994 management of the resort was taken over by the Holiday Inn chain.

HOW TO GET THERE
By Air
Ansett, ✆13 1300, Qantas, ✆13 1313, and Transtate, ✆131 528, fly directly to Hamilton Island.
By Sea
Blue Ferries (Fantasea Cruises), ✆4946 5111, operate a service to Hamilton from Shute Harbour for $38 return.

VISITOR INFORMATION
An extensive website is provided at ☞www.hamiltonisland.com.au

The Hamilton Island Resort can be contacted on ✆4946 9999 or ✆1800 075 110.

ACCOMMODATION AND SERVICES
There are four different types of accommodation from which to choose, all of which are part of the *Hamilton Island Resort*, ✆4946 9999 or ✆1800 075 110.

Beach Club Resort - 55 boutique-style rooms on Catseye Beach.

Reef View Hotel - 368 rooms and suites from Garden View to Presidential.

Whitsunday Holiday Apartments - 168 one bedroom apartments and 13 two bedroom apartments.

Coconut Palms bungalows and lodges - 50 freestanding Polynesian-style bungalows.

Resort facilities are: 6 swimming pools, 16 restaurants and take-aways, bars, shops and boutiques, tennis courts, squash courts, a gymnasium, aerobic classes, mini golf, live entertainment, parasailing, waterskiing, sailboards, SCUBA diving and lessons, catamarans and a free Kids' Club.

Room facilities are: private balcony, air-conditioning, fans, tea/coffee making facilities, ironing facilities, refrigerator and mini bar, colour TV, IDD/STD telephone and hairdryer.

Tariffs for a double room per night are:

Coconut Palms - ✪$200

Reef View - ✪$200-325

Whitsunday -   ✪$250
Beach Club -   ✪$350

The above rates are room only, and include use of most facilities. All other activities, meals and drinks are at the visitor's expense.

Bookings can be made online or through the resort. Credit cards accepted: all major cards.

POINTS OF INTEREST

The resort is actually a small town with shops, restaurants and a 135-berth marina. There are a few walking tracks on the undeveloped parts of the island, and the main one leads up to Passage Peak (230m) the highest point on the island. To get around the island, you can rent a golf buggy and drive yourself. Hamilton even has island bus tours that operate daily.

There is a **Fauna Park** at the northern end of the island, with native animals, crocodiles and performing cockatoos.

4WD safari tours, go-karts and skirmish are further activities.

DIVING

H2O Sportz, Front Street, Hamilton Island, ℰ4946 9888, is the only diving operation on Hamilton Island. A PADI 5-star Dive Centre, it has all the services expected of a top dive facility. There is a wide range of diving options ranging from half-day trips to nearby fringing reefs, day trips on specialist dive boats, and large catamarans that sail to the Outer Reef.

H2O Sportz offer daily trips to the Outer Barrier Reef and visits such sites as Hook, Hardy, Black and Bait Reefs and the Whitsunday Island area. These are all Marine National Parks and offer some of the best diving in the area.

The one-day introduction program, Discover Scuba, costs ✪$185 and includes 2 escorted reef dives. A four-day open water course, with four-dives, is $450. The Advanced Diver Course is $400, with a 2-3 day duration and five ocean dives.

Mackay

HOOK ISLAND

Map F

LOCATION AND CHARACTERISTICS

Hook Island has an area of 53 sq km, some great beaches and some of the best diving sites in the Whitsundays, but it has one of the smallest resorts. The focus here is on the budget market, with a choice between camping sites, beachfront cabins and backpacker dorms.

Hook Island has two long, narrow bays on its southern end - Macona Inlet and Nara Inlet. Macona has a National Park camping site, and Nara has caves with Aboriginal wall paintings.

There is a variety of wildlife on the island, but one that can prove quite pesky is the large goanna. These have been known to chew through canvas to get to campers' stores.

HOW TO GET THERE

By Air

Transfer by seaplane is an option, and it is best to enquire when making reservations at the resort for the best current prices.

By Sea

A catamaran service departs daily from Airlie Beach.

VISITOR INFORMATION

The website is ☞www.hookislandresort.com.au and the email address is ✐enquiries@hookis.com

The Wilderness Resort can answer any further enquiries, ☏4946 9380.

ACCOMMODATION AND SERVICES

The low-key **Wilderness Resort** has only three styles of accommodation - camping, cabins and dorms.

Resort facilities are: bar, coffee shop, gift shop, barbecue area, paddle skis and an on-site scuba instructor.

Beachfront cabins have private showers and a refrigerator, but toilet and cooking facilities are shared.

Dorms are shared accommodation facilities.

Camp sites are on the beachfronts, and have barbecues available for use.
Tariffs for a double per night are:

Cabins -   ✪$95 adults, $20 children

Dorms -   ✪$20 adults, $15 children

Camp Sites -   ✪$13 adults, $7 children

Reservations can be made through the Hook Island Wilderness Resort ✆4946 9380 or by phoning ✆4946 9925.

POINTS OF INTEREST

The island is home to an underwater observatory that has an abundance of colourful corals and marine life. Though with so many trips available to the Outer Reef and the modern semi-submersible craft that tour operators use, you have to wonder why anyone would want to visit an underwater observatory. Still, it is popular with many visitors.

DIVING

The northern end of Hook Island has some good diving and snorkelling sites - Pinnacle Point, Manta Ray Bay, Butterfly Bay and Alcyonaria Point. The resort can organise reef trips.

DAYDREAM ISLAND

Map F

LOCATION AND CHARACTERISTICS

Daydream is a small island with an area of just 17ha. It is a little over 1km long and no more than a couple of hundred metres at its widest point, but it has one of the largest resorts.

Originally known as West Molle, the island is the closest resort island to Shute Harbour. It was first settled in the 1880s by graziers, but the first resort was opened by Paddy Murray, who had purchased the island in 1933 and changed its name to Daydream after his boat.

Reg Ansett (later Sir Reginald), of airline fame, bought the resort in 1947 and ran it until 1953 when he pulled the whole lot down and transferred it to Hayman Island.

Mackay

In the mid-1960s, a resort was established under the leadership of Bernie Elsey and it operated until destroyed by a cyclone in 1970. During this time Daydream's reputation was anything but squeaky clean - perhaps the 60s was not the decade to introduce topless bathing or illegal gambling.

The Jennings Group Ltd spent $100 million on a new complex at the northern end of the island and opened it in December 1990. Previous resorts had been at the southern end, but that part now has a Beach Club, with a nice sandy beach, a swimming pool, a bar, shops and a cafe. This is where all water activities are based, and the facilities can be used by resort guests and people on day trips from other islands and the mainland.

HOW TO GET THERE

By Air
After flying to Proserpine airport, a coach will transfer guests to Shute Harbour to connect with the water taxi to the island.

Flights can also be made to Hamilton Island, followed by a (✪$38 return) trip with Blue Ferries to Daydream.

By Sea
Blue Ferries, ✆4946 5111, have services from Shute Harbour to Daydream for ✪$16 return.

VISITOR INFORMATION
Contact the resort on ✆4948 8488 or ✆1800 075 040 (reservations). The official web page is found at ✑www.daydream.net.au

ACCOMMODATION AND SERVICES
Daydream Island Resort accommodation is divided into three categories, all of which can accommodate up to 4 people: Ocean View Room, Garden View Room and Sunlover Room. Interconnecting rooms for larger families are available on request.

Resort facilities are: 3 restaurants, bakery/coffee shop, 4 bars, live entertainment, disco, spas, sauna, 2 swimming pools, 2 spas, gymnasium, aerobics, 2 tennis courts, windsurfing, catamaran sailing, paddle skis, snorkelling scuba diving and tuition, outer Reef excursions, waterskiing, parasailing, tour desk, laundry/ironing facilities, Kids' Club and child care.

Room facilities are: private bathrooms, mini bar, iron/board, hairdryer, tea/coffee making facilities, refrigerator, air-conditioning, colour TV, in-house movies, IDD/STD telephone, radio and daily cleaning services.

Tariffs for a double room per night are:

Garden View -   ✪$280
Ocean View -   ✪$320
Sunlover -   ✪$375

The above rates include breakfast and use of most facilities. Not included are any sports that require fuel.

Reservations can be made online or through the resorts phone booking service, ✆1 800 075 040.

POINTS OF INTEREST

DIVING

Sunlover's Beach, at the north-eastern end of the island, behind the resort, has a 50m strip of sand and some good coral offshore for snorkellers. The Whitsunday tidal range does not affect Daydream as much as the other islands.

The Resort dive shop offers courses, and day cruises to Hardy Reef, about 50km offshore.

BRAMPTON ISLAND

Map J

LOCATION AND CHARACTERISTICS

Brampton is not strictly in the Whitsunday region. It is part of the Cumberland Group of Islands about 32km north-east of Mackay, at the entrance to the Whitsunday Passage. The island is a National Park, with an area of 4.6 sq km, and has unspoilt bush, lush tropical foliage, swaying coconut palms and many stunning and secluded

Mackay

beaches. It is connected to Carlisle Island and to Pelican Island by sand bars that can be crossed at low tide.

A mountainous island with lush forests, nature trails, kangaroos and emus, Brampton also has seven sandy beaches and is surrounded by coral reefs. The walk around the island is about 7km, takes around three hours, and is best done in a clockwise direction. There is a walk up to the island's highest point, Brampton Peak, beginning near the resort golf course and the round trip takes about two hours. Both walks offer great views.

Although Captain Cook was in the area, he either didn't see Brampton or he wasn't interested, because the island was not named and surveyed until 1879.

In the early 1900s the Queensland government used the island as a nursery for palm trees, which accounts for the abundance of those trees now.

The Busuttin family moved to Brampton in 1916 to breed chinchilla rabbits, and when this proved unsuccessful they tried their hand at raising goats and horses for the British Army in India. In 1933 the family opened a resort, but they kept the livestock side going until just after the war, when they needed more space for visitors. The Busuttins sold the resort in 1959, and it went through several pairs of hands before becoming the property of the Roylen group, who still handle the boat transfers from Mackay to Brampton.

The island is a 45 minute cruise from the Great Barrier Reef, but you can see underwater coral gardens and myriads of tropical fish off Brampton's East Beach.

HOW TO GET THERE

By Air

Transtate Airlines make regular flights to Brampton, ✆131 528. The cost one-way is ✪$85 adults and $40 children.

By Sea

The *Spirit of Roylen* launch, ✆4955 3066, departs daily from Mackay. Return fares are ✪$60 adults and $30 children.

VISITOR INFORMATION

The contact number for the resort is ✆4951 4097, and the website is 👁www.bramptonislandresort.com

ACCOMMODATION AND SERVICES

Brampton Island Resort, ✆4951 4097, has three styles of accommodation - 36 Ocean View Rooms, 56 Palm Rooms and 16 Carlisle Rooms.

Resort facilities are: restaurant, cocktail bar, two swimming pools, spa, games room, tennis courts, cafe, Kids' Club, surf skis, gymnasium, tube rides, golf, waterskiing, catamaran sailing, sailboarding, beach volleyball, snorkelling, cruising and coral viewing, Barrier Reef trips and EFTPOS.

Room facilities are: balcony or verandah, tea and coffee making facilities, refrigerator, colour TV, in-house movies, IDD/STD telephone, radio, air-conditioning and a daily cleaning service.

Tariffs for one night per person/twin share are:

Ocean View - ✪$230 adult (child 3-14 years sharing with 2 adults - free)

Palm - ✪$200 adult (child - as above)

Carlisle - ✪$180 (child - as above)

The above rates include a full buffet breakfast, four course smorgasbord lunch and four-course dinner.

Maximum occupancy of all rooms is 3 persons (child is counted as a person).

Additional to the tariff are: Great Barrier Reef cruises, Great Barrier Reef flights, bullet rides, fishing trips, forest walks (day), Melaleuca Tour on Carlisle Island, scuba diving lessons and trips, water skiing, Whitsunday Island Cruises. Reservations can be made through the resort by phone or online. Credit cards accepted: Visa, MasterCard, Bankcard, Diners Club, American Express.

Mackay

Eating Out

The **Bluewater Restaurant** is the dining room where main meals are taken. There is also the **Bluewater Lounge** for post- and pre-dinner drinks, with entertainment. The **Saltwater Cafe & Bar** is ☉open from 11am-5pm and serves sandwiches, salads and light meals. This is where the day trippers usually stop for a bite to eat.

POINTS OF INTEREST

DIVING

There is nothing at Brampton itself to excite divers, but cruises from Mackay to Credlin Reef aboard the *Spirit of Roylen*, ✆4955 3066, call in at Brampton to pick up and set down. Credlin Reef is in the Hydrographers Passage area, and there is a permanent pontoon over the reef, an underwater observatory and a semi-submersible. Resort diving courses are conducted on board the *Spirit of Roylen* in transit to Credlin Reef, or at the Resort by special arrangements.

MACKAY

Map G

Population 58,600

Mackay is a coastal city, on the banks of the Pioneer River, 975km (606 miles) north of Brisbane.

CLIMATE

Average temperatures: January max 31C (88F) - min 22C (72F); July max 23C (73F) - min 10C (50F). Average annual rainfall - 1672mm (66 ins), with over 1000mm (39 ins) falling January-March. The driest months are June-November.

CHARACTERISTICS

Mackay is surrounded by miles and miles of sugarcane fields, which give the city its title of Sugar Capital of Australia. The district produces about one-third of Australia's total sugar crop, which is exported through the Port of Mackay.

Tram tracks meander through the fields, for the miniature engines that transport the cane to one of the seven sugar mills in the district. In some places the fields are torched between June and December, just before harvesting, and the night skies turn red with the reflections from the fires. These days this method is more frequently replaced by 'green harvesting', which involves cutting rather than burning. See under *Points of Interest* for details of a sugar farm tour.

North-east of Mackay, just off the coast from Shute Harbour, is the Whitsunday Group of Islands containing some of the most popular of the resort islands of the Great Barrier Reef. Although these islands are not coral cays, the scenery is similar to those featuring in your dreams of lazing on a palm-fringed beach on a tropical island.

The beautiful Eungella National Park, 84km inland from Mackay, has graded tracks leading through rainforest to waterfalls and cool pools (*see separate listing*).

HOW TO GET THERE

By Air
Ansett, ✆13 1300, fly from/to Adelaide, Brisbane, Bundaberg, Burnie, Canberra, Darwin, Devonport, Gladstone, Gold Coast, Hobart, Launceston, Melbourne, Mount Isa, Perth, Rockhampton, Sydney and Tamworth.

The Qantas regional airlines of Airlink and Sunstate service Mackay, ✆131 313.

Flight West also operates routes to Mackay, ✆1300 130 092.

By Bus
Greyhound Pioneer, ✆13 2030, stops at Mackay on its Brisbane/Cairns route.

McCaffertys, ✆13 1499, also operates a Brisbane/Mackay service which takes the inland route from Rockhampton.

Mackay

By Rail

Queensland Rail Travel Trains operate The Sunlander, The Queenslander and The Spirit of Tropics from Brisbane throughout the week, contact ✆13 2235.

The number for the Mackay Railway Station is ✆4952 7418.

By Road

From Brisbane, via the Bruce Highway, 975km (606 miles).
Mackay is 1079km (670 miles) south of Cairns.

VISITOR INFORMATION

Mackay Tourism and Development Bureau Ltd is in 'The Mill', 320 Nebo Road, ✆4952 2677, and they are ☉open Mon-Fri 9am-5pm, Sat-Sun 9am-4pm. Their email is ✉mtdb@mackay.net.au

LOCAL TRANSPORT

Car Hire

The following companies operate in the area.

Avis, Mackay Airport, ✆4951 1266.
AAA Rental-U-Drive, 6 Endevour Street, ✆4957 5606.
Budget Rent-A-Car, 19B Juliet Street, ✆4951 1400
Thrifty Car Rental, 3 Mangrove Road, ✆4957 3677.
Mackay Economy Rentals, 139 Sydney Street, ✆4953 1616.
Hertz Rentals, Mackay Airport, ✆4951 4685.
Network Rentals, 196 Victoria Street, ✆4953 1022
Cut Rate Rentals, 105 Alfred Street, ✆4953 1616

Public Transport

Buses service the Mackay area on weekdays only, not on public holidays, ✆4957 8416 for timetable information from Mackay City Buses.

Taxis

Taxi Transit, Victoria Street, ✆4951 4990.
Mackay Taxis, Victoria Street, ✆13 1008.

ACCOMMODATION

Mackay has a wide range of accommodation, from international resort hotels and motels, to caravan parks and camping grounds. Here is a selection with prices for a double room per night, which should be used as a guide only. The telephone area code is 07.

Ocean International Hotel, I Bridge Street, ✆4957 2044. 46 rooms, licensed restaurant, swimming pool, spa, sauna, putting green, barbecue - ✪$140-221.

Four Dice, 166 Nebo Road, ✆4951 1555. 34 units, 2 suites, licensed restaurant, undercover parking, pool - ✪$102.

Marco Polo Motel, 46 Nebo Road, ✆4951 2700. 30 units, licensed restaurant, swimming pool, spa, sauna, gym - ✪$92.

Shakespeare International, 309 Shakespeare Street, ✆4953 1111. 37 units, 17 suites, licensed restaurant, swimming pool, spa, barbecue - ✪$85.

White Lace Motor Inn, 73 Nebo Road, ✆4951 4466. 36 units, licensed restaurant, swimming pool, spa - ✪$79-109.

Sugar City, 66 Nebo Road, ✆4968 4150 or 1800 645 525 (toll free). 21 units, barbecue, licensed restaurant, playground, room service, car parking, pool - ✪$76-84.

Alara Motor Inn, 52 Nebo Road, ✆4951 2699. 34 units, licensed restaurant, swimming pool, spa, sauna - ✪$75- 98.

Ocean Resort Village, 5 Bridge Street, ✆4951 3200 or 1800 075 144 (toll free). 34 units, kiosk, tennis half- court, undercover parking, 2 pools - ✪$75.

Coral Sands Motel, 44 MacAlister Street, ✆4951 1244. 46 units, 2 suites, licensed restaurant (closed Sun), swimming pool, sauna, barbecue - ✪$66-74.

Country Plaza Motor Inn, 40 Nebo Road, ✆4957 6526. 38 units, licensed restaurant, undercover parking, pool, spa - ✪$63-65.

Paradise Lodge Motel, 19 Peel Street, ✆4951 3644. 12 units, undercover parking - ✪$52-56.

Pioneer Villa, 30 Nebo Road, ☎4951 1288. 18 units, licensed restaurant, swimming pool, barbecue - ✪$50-65.

Hi Way Units, Nebo Road, cnr Webberley Street, ☎4952 1800. 7 units, undercover parking, swimming pool - ✪$50.

Bona Vista Motel, cnr Malcomson Street & Norris Road, ☎4942 2211. 18 units, licensed restaurant, swimming pool, barbecue - ✪$38-45.

Boomerang, South Nebo Road, ☎4952 1755. 23 units, unlicensed restaurant, playground, pool - ✪$38-40.

Budget Accommodation

The places listed below offer double rooms at less than $50 per night:

Mackay Townhouse, 73 Victoria Street, ☎4957 6985.

International Lodge, 40 MacAlister Street, ☎4951 1022.

Austral Hotel, 189 Victoria Street, ☎4951 3288.

Taylors Hotel, cnr Wood & Alfred Streets, ☎4957 2500.

There is a **Youth Hostel** at 32 Peel Street, ☎4951 3728. 6 rooms at ✪$17 per person twin share.

Northern Beaches

Approximately 15 minutes drive north of Mackay.

Dolphin Heads Resort, Beach Road, Dolphin Heads, ☎4954 9666 or ☎1800 075 088 (free call). 2 units, licensed restaurant, swimming pool and spa, tennis court - ✪$165.

Ko Huna Beach, Homestead Bay Avenue, Bucasia, ☎5954 8555 or ☎1800 075 128 (toll free). 60 units, 2 licensed restaurants, swimming pool and spa, mini golf, tennis, watersport activities - ✪$98-130.

The Shores, 9 Pacific Drive, Blacks Beach, ☎4954 9444. 36 units, cooking facilities, undercover parking, 2 swimming pools, spa, tennis court - ✪$85-145.

Blue Pacific Village, 24 Bourke Street, Blacks Beach, ☎4954 9090. 38 units, licensed restaurant, barbecue, playground, undercover parking, cooking facilities, swimming pool, half-court tennis, heated pool, spa - ✪$83-130.

Pacific Palms Beachfront Units, Symons Avenue, Bucasia Beach, ©4954 6277. 6 units, cooking facilities, swimming pool, undercover parking - ✪$62-69.

La Solana, 15 Pacific Drive, Blacks Beach, ©4954 9544. 12 units, barbecue, playground, cooking facilities, swimming pool, half-court tennis - ✪$55-85.

Tropic Heart Units, 64 Waverley Street, Bucasia, ©4954 6965. 7 units, barbecue, undercover parking, cooking facilities, swimming pool - ✪$44-65.

Hibiscus Coast
Approximately 40-45 minutes drive north of Mackay
See under *Cape Hillsborough* and *Halliday Bay*, which have separate listings.

Sarina
Approximately 30 minutes drive south of Mackay.
Sarina Motor Inn, Bruce Highway, ©4943 1431 or ©1800 248 087. 16 units, licensed restaurant, undercover parking, room service, pool - ✪$50-60.

Tramway, 110 Broad Street, ©4956 2244. 12 units, cooking facilities, playground, undercover parking, pool - ✪$48-60.

Tandara, Broad Street, ©4956 1323. 15 units, licensed restaurant, undercover parking - ✪$42-45.

Caravan Parks
Beach Tourist Park, 8 Petrie Street, Illawong Beach, ©4957 4021 or 1800 645 111 (tollfree). (No pets allowed) 150 sites, playground, kiosk, pool - powered sites ✪$18 for two, villas $50-52, cabins $40-50 for two.

Andergrove Caravan Park, Beaconsfield Road, Andergrove, ©4942 4922. (Pets allowed on application) 160 sites, barbecue, playground, pool - powered sites ✪$16 for two, on-site vans $28 for two, cabins $40 for two.

Tropical Caravan Park Melanesian Village, Bruce Highway, ✆4952 1211. (Pets allowed on application) 170 sites, barbecue, playground, kiosk, pool - powered sites ✪$15 for two, on-site vans $28 for two, villas $45-50 for two, units $40-44 for two.

Premier Van Park, 152 Nebo Road, ✆4957 6976. (No pets allowed) 42 sites, barbecue, kiosk pool - powered sites ✪$14 for two, cabins $30-35 for two.

EATING OUT

Most of the motels have licensed restaurants, and many hotels serve inexpensive counter meals. Here are a few restaurants that you might like to try.

Pippi's Italian Restaurant, cnr Palmer & Grendon Streets, ✆4951 1376. BYO, Italian & Mediterranean, open Tues-Sat from 5.30pm.

Romeo & Juliet's Restaurant, 309 Shakespeare Street, ✆4953 1111. Licensed, a la carte - fresh local produce and fine Aussie wines are the specialties. Open nightly from 6.30pm.

The Beachhouse Seafood Restaurant, 2 Ocean Avenue, Slade Point, ✆4955 4733. Metres from the water's edge. Generous platters and Live Mud Crab Tank. Open for dinner seven nights, lunch Thursday, Friday and Sunday.

Valencia Restaurant, 44 MacAlister Street, at the Coral Sands Motel, ✆4951 1244. Licensed, a la carte, piano bar - open for dinner from 6.30pm, and for lunch Mon-Fri.

Toong Tong Thai Restaurant, 10 Sydney Street, Mackay, ✆4957 8051. Dinner 7 days from 5.30pm, lunch Mon-Fri 11.30am-2.30pm.

McDonald's is at the corner of Hicks Road and the Bruce Highway, ✆4942 3999. Pizza Hut has a free delivery service Mon-Thurs 4-11pm, Fri-Sun noon-11pm, ✆4957 2481.

ENTERTAINMENT

If you fancy seeing a **movie**, head for the cinema complex in Gordon Street, ✆4957 3515.

Mackay

For some **live entertainment** contact the *Mackay Entertainment Centre*, also in Gordon Street, ℭ4957 1757 or ℭ1800 646 574, to find out about current shows.

The *Conservatorium of Music*, 418 Shakespeare Street, has regular classical and jazz concerts, often featuring overseas artists, ℭ4957 3727. For night owls, there are a few **night clubs** where you can dance to the wee small hours:

Whitz End, The Whitsunday Hotel, 176 Victoria Street, ℭ4957 2811.

The Blue Moose Nightclub, 144 Victoria Street, ℭ4951 2611. ⏰Open Wed-Sun nights.

The Balcony, 144 Victoria Street, ℭ4957 2241.

Katie O'Reilly's Irish Bar & Restaurant, 38 Sydney Street, ℭ4953 3522.

The Saloon Bar, 99 Victoria Street, ℭ4957 7220.

If you are in town on a Thursday night you might like to go to the greyhound racing at the *Mackay Showground* in Milton Street, ℭ4951 1680.

SHOPPING

Centrepoint Shopping Centre, ℭ4957 2229, is in Victoria Street, in the heart of the city, where you will also find some good street shopping.

Caneland Shoppingtown, ℭ4951 3311, is in Mangrove Road.

Mt Pleasant Shopping Centre, Phillip Street, North Mackay, is more convenient for those staying to the north of the city.

Weekend markets are held as follows:

The *Foundry Markets* on Harbour Road - ⏰Thursday, Sat-Sun 8am-4pm.

Mackay Showground Markets in Milton Road - ⏰Sat 8am-1pm.

Victoria Street Markets - ⏰Sun 8.30am-12.30pm.

On the first Sunday of every month *Paxtons Markets* are held in River Street ⏰9am-1pm, and on most long weekends the *Eungella Markets* are staged at Dalrymple Heights Oval.

Mackay

ARTS & CRAFTS

Pioneer Potters in Swayne Street, North Mackay, ✆4957 6255, has a good selection of handmade local pottery and sculpture. It is ⏰open Wed and Sat 10am-4pm.

The Beach Pottery, 6 Blacks Beach Road, Blacks Beach, offers functional stoneware pottery by local potters. It is ⏰open Mon-Thurs 10am-5pm, and weekends by arrangement.

Bucasia Gardens and Gifts, Bucasia Road, about ten minutes drive past Mt Pleasant Shopping Centre, has a wide selection of local pottery, crafts, dried flowers and giftware. It is ⏰open daily 9.30am-5pm, ✆4954 8134, and also has a coffee shop, plants and pots.

Homebush Store Pottery & Craft Gallery is situated 26km south-west of Mackay in an historic building, Sunnyside Road. Opening in the early 1900 as the local store for the people of Homebush and surrounding areas, it has now been restored and is operated as a pottery workshop. Also available are works of art, fibre arts, woodturned objects, hand painted T-shirts and handmade cane baskets. The Gallery is ⏰open Fri-Tues 9am-5pm, ✆4959 7339.

POINTS OF INTEREST

John Mackay discovered the Pioneer River Valley in 1860, but he named the river the Mackay. He returned with stock and registered "Greenmount" the first pastoral run in the district in 1862. Others followed and the settlement was named Mackay in his honour. The river's name, however, had to be changed to Pioneer because there was already a Mackay River.

It was only a few years before sugar became the main industry, pioneered by the efforts of John Spiller, T. Henry Fitzgerald and John Ewen Davidson. Nowadays Mackay Harbour is home to the world's largest bulk sugar terminal.

The port for Mackay was originally on the river, but because of the enormous tides (around 6.5m), a new port was built on the coast.

Tourism Mackay have put together a *City Walking Tour* that visits the historic buildings, including the Police Station (1885), Court House,

Commonwealth Bank (1880), Town Hall (1912), Holy Trinity Church, Masonic Temple, National Bank, Mercury Building, Pioneer Shire Chambers, Post Office and Customs House (1901).

The closest beach to the city is **Harbour Beach**, on the southern side of the outer harbour wall. It has a children's playground, toilets and shady picnic areas, and is patrolled during summer by the Mackay Surf Club.

Queen's Park Orchid House, cnr Gordon & Goldsmith Streets, has an excellent display of native and foreign orchids.

Port Mackay at sunrise

Mackay

Illawong Fauna Sanctuary, at Illawong Beach, 4km from Mackay centre, is a beachfront family recreation area amid tropical landscaping. There are kangaroos roaming free, a swimming pool, trampoline, video games and full catering facilities, as well as crocodiles (not roaming free). Feeding times are 9am, 11.30am and 3.30pm. For further information, ✆4959 1777. The sanctuary is ⏱open 9am-6pm daily, and until 10pm on Friday night.

You can get a good panoramic view of the city and the countryside from the **Mt Oscar Lookout** in Norris Road, North Mackay.

Tours of the **Racecourse Sugar Mill**, Peak Downs Highway, are conducted during the crushing season, from June to November, ✆4953 8276 for more information.

Polstone Sugar Farm Tours, Masotti's Road, Homebush, adjacent to Orchid Way, conduct a 2 hour tour covering the history, equipment and process of growing and preparing sugar cane for the mill. Costs, including refreshments, are ✪$12 adults and $6 children, ✆4959 7298. North of Mackay are several popular beach resorts.

Blacks Beach is approximately 6km in length, and is probably the best beach in the area for swimming and fishing. **Bucasia** and **Eimeo** beaches are in the semi-rural area, about a 10 minute drive north of Mackay, and are long sandy beaches that are safe for swimming and have good play areas for kids. They also offer good views of the countryside and off-shore islands.

Beaches

Illawong (Far Beach) and **Iluka** (Town Beach) offer views of Flat and Round Top Islands and Dalrymple Bay/Hay Point coal loading terminal.

Harbour Beach has a surf lifesaving patrol, toilets, adventure playground and picnic area.

Lamberts Beach has a lookout that provides island views.

Blacks Beach is a long secluded beach with picnic facilities.

Dolphin Heads has accommodation available.

Eimeo Beach has a small picnic area next to an avenue of century old mango trees.

Sunset Beach has a shaded foreshore picnic area.

Bucasia Beach has a summer swimming enclosure, picnic area and views to Dolphin Heads and islands.

Shoal Point Beach has a picnic area, toilets and lookout. The Esplanade offers views of islands, Cape Hillsborough and Hibiscus Coast, and there is a causeway to Little Green Island.

SOUTH OF MACKAY

Twenty-five kilometres south of Mackay, at Hay Point, is the **Dalrymple Bay Coal Terminal Complex**, the largest coal export facility in the southern hemisphere. The wharves stretch 3.8km out to sea, and coal trains up to 2km long arrive at the port daily. The Port Administration Building has recorded information and a viewing platform, ✆4943 8444.

The **Big Prawn** is at Lot 1, Grasstree Beach Road, Grasstree Beach, and is the only commercial hatchery in Australia that is open to the public.

The sugar town of **Sarina** is 37km south of Mackay. It has a population of around 9,000, some picturesque scenery, and some excellent beaches. *(See also separate listing.)*

Cape Palmerston National Park is 80km south of Mackay and has 4WD only access. It offers long sandy beaches, palm forests, fresh-water lagoons and large stands of melaleuca. Attractions include Ince Bay to the north, Temple Island and the volcanic plug of Mt Funnel. There is camping, but facilities are very basic.

Beaches

Campwin Beach, 8.5km from Sarina, is home to a rich fishing and prawning industry. Boat launching and mooring facilities are available and there is easy access to nearby islands.

Armstrong Beach is 9.5km from Sarina and has a picnic and camping, and an orchid nursery that is open by appointment only.

Sarina Beach, 13km from Sarina, has a picnic area, store, boat ramp, and a surf lifesaving patrol. Coral Lookout is at the southern end of the beach.

Mackay

Grasstree Beach, 13km from Sarina, has a picnic area and boat ramp in a wide sheltered bay.

Salonika Beach, 24km from Sarina, is a quiet sandy beach with an inland lagoon teeming with birdlife.

Halftide Beach, 28km from Sarina, is home to the Tug Boat Harbour that services Hay Point Coal Terminal.

NORTH OF MACKAY

Cape Hillsborough National Park, 45km (28 miles) north-east of Mackay, covers 830ha and features a variety of vegetation, elevated lookouts and peaceful beaches. It is not unusual to see a couple of kangaroos lazing on the beach undisturbed by humans doing the same thing.

Cathu State Forest is 70km (44 miles) north of Mackay. Drive along the Bruce Highway to 3km north of Yalboroo, turn left and continue for 12km (8 miles) along the gravel road to the Forestry Office. Within the forest is the Jaxut State Forest Park which has shaded picnic areas with friendly kangaroos, camping facilities and toilets.

Midge Point is reached by turning right off the Bruce Highway at Bloomsbury, and travelling 18km through the Condor Hill to the village of Midgetown. Named after a small survey vessel, the *Midge*, in the early 1920s, this area has been 'discovered' by developers, and has become a tourist destination.

Beaches

Roughly 25km north of Mackay, turn right onto Seaforth Road then travel 20km to the **Hibiscus Coast**. This includes the beachside settlements of Seaforth, Halliday Bay, Ball Bay and Cape Hillsborough. These beaches are all nesting sites for green and flatback turtles who lay their eggs during the three month period from October each year. The baby turtles hatch between late January and early April.

Halliday Bay has a sandy beach swimming enclosure, accommodation and a restaurant. It is reached from Cape Hillsborough Road.

Mackay

Seaforth is 48km north-east of Mackay, and offers camping and picnic facilities overlooking the beach.

Belmunda Bay is reached by turning right about 5km along the Cape Hillsborough Road. The bay has secluded beaches with several fishing shacks. After rain has fallen, the nearby freshwater lakes are visited by crowds of water birds, including the brolga.

FESTIVALS

The Sugartime Festival is held in the first week in September each year.

SPORTS

Golf

There are three golf courses within 40km of Mackay city:

Mackay Golf Club, Bucasia Road, Mackay, ✆4942 1362.

The Valley Golf Club, Leichhardt Street, Mirani, ✆4959 1277.

Sarina Golf Club, Golf Links Road, Sarina, ✆4956 1761.

Swimming

The *Memorial Swimming Pool*, Milton Street, is near Caneland Shopping Centre. It is ⏰open Tues, Thurs and Fri 5am-8.45pm, Wed, Sat and Sun 5am-6pm (closed June and early July).

Whitsunday Waterworld, Harbour Road, Mackay, ✆4955 6466, is a complex with waterslides, mini golf, pinball, video machines and kiosk. It is ⏰open Sat-Sun and school holidays 10am-10pm.

Indoor Sports

BG's Sports Centre on the Bruce Highway south of the City Gates, is one of the largest indoor recreational and fitness centres in Australia. It offers tenpin bowling, roller skating, squash and many other sports, ✆4952 1509. It is ⏰open daily 9am-midnight.

Diving

The Diver Training Centre, ✆4955 4228, has a dive shop by the sea next to the departure point for Roylen Cruises, where you can hire snorkel and scuba gear. They also have 5-day dive courses.

Mackay

Barnes Reefdiving, 153 Victoria Street, ©4951 1472, offer diving trips to the Great Barrier Reef on Mon, Wed and Fri; Reef and Wreck Dive Trips on Tues; and Island Dive Trips on Thurs.

Mackay Diving, 1 Mangrove Road, ©4951 1640, also offer gear hire and diving lessons.

TOURS AND CRUISES

Natural North Discovery Tours, 11 Rafelo Drive, Farleigh, ©4952 2677 or ©4959 8360. Eungella National Park Tour - daily - 10 hours duration - ✪$70 adults, $50 children and $205 for families.

The Great Barrier Reef can be reached from Mackay by sea and air. Credlin Reef, one of the 2100 reefs that make up this coral colony, is only 2 to 3 hours from Mackay Harbour by high speed catamaran. There is a shaded pontoon, underwater viewing area and a seasub that make for excellent snorkelling, scuba diving and coral viewing.

Bushy Atoll, a half-hour seaplane flight from Mackay airport, is the only quay on the entire Reef to have an enclosed lagoon.

Elizabeth E II Coral Cruises, 102 Goldsmith Street, Mackay, ©4957 4281, offer trips from two to 21 days aboard their specially built monohull dive and fishing boat, *Elizabeth E II*. The boat is stabilised and has the latest navigation aids, as well as 240v throughout and a 110v charging system.

Accommodation for 12 to 28 passengers are in one double, 12 twin and two triple berths with en-suite facilities and unlimited fresh water. All meals are chef-prepared and snacks, weights, air and tanks are included in the charter costs.

Mackay Adventure Cruises, 320 Nebo Road, ©4952 2677. High-speed catamaran transport to the Credlin Reef pontoon for coral viewing.

Whitsunday Dreamer, ©4946 6611. Snorkelling and fishing. Stopovers to Daydream Island, Long Island and Sun Lovers coral reef.

Roylen Cruises, Harbour Road, ©4955 3066, have daily cruises to Brampton Island; Sat, Sun & Wed cruises to Lindeman and Hamilton Islands; Mon, Wed & Fri cruises to Credlin Reef; and 5-day luxury cruises through the Whitsunday Islands and to the Great Barrier Reef,

Mackay

all departing from the outer harbour. The 5-day cruise departs every Monday 1pm and returns Friday 4pm.

SCENIC FLIGHTS

Horizon Airways, Casey Avenue, Mackay, ©4957 2446. Half-hour flights over Mackay.

Air Pioneer, Old Airport, Casey Avenue, Mackay, ©4957 6661. Offers flights to a coral atoll, then onto a glass-bottomed boat for touring plus snorkelling.

Whitsunday Helicopter Group, Mackay Airport, ©4953 3061. Joy flights over the Barrier Reef.

Fredericksons Air Services, 25 Norman Drive, Yeppoon, ©4938 3404. Includes 2-hour flights to Bushy Reef.

Loading sugar cane near Mackay

Mackay

MACKAY TO ROCKHAMPTON
SARINA

Map J

Population 9000

LOCATION AND CHARACTERISTICS

The town of Sarina is 37km (23 miles) south of Mackay, and 296km (185 miles) north of Rockhampton, on the Bruce Highway. It is yet another sugar town in the area, cradled by rainforest and the Conners Range mountains. 13km (8 miles) to the north east is a charming little village by the sea, Sarina Beach. Fishing and snorkelling is popular in the tropical islands and reefs close to the mainland.

HOW TO GET THERE

By Car

Sarina is on the Bruce Highway, 37km south of Mackay and 296km north of Rockhampton.

VISITOR INFORMATION

Helpful local information is provided by the Sarina Tourist Art & Craft Centre, Lot 3 Bruce Highway, ✆4956 2251.

ACCOMMODATION AND SERVICES

Sarina has a good range of accommodation in hotels, caravan parks and beachfront motels.

Sarina Beach, The Esplanade, Sarina Beach, ✆4956 6266. 17 units, licensed restaurant, playground, room service, tennis half-court, pool - ✪$58-85.

Sarina Motor Inn, Bruce Highway, Sarina, ✆4943 1431 or ✆1800 248 087. 16 units, licensed restaurant, undercover parking, room service, pool - ✪$50-60.

Sandpiper, Owen Jenkins Drive, Sarina Beach, ✆4956 6130. 23 units, barbecue, undercover parking, pool, spa - ✪$48-75.

Tramway, 110 Broad Street, Sarina, ✆4956 2244. 12 units, barbecue, undercover parking, playground, pool - ✪$48-60.

Tandara, Broad Street, Sarina, ©4956 1323. 15 units, licensed restaurant, undercover parking - ✪$42-45.

Caravan Parks

Sarina Beach Caravan Park, Owen Jenkins Drive, Sarina Beach, ©4956 6130. 31 sites - powered sites ✪$15.50.

Sarina Palms Caravan Village, 11 Heron Street, Sarina, ©4956 1892. 38 sites, kiosk - powered sites ✪$12 for two, cabins $25-29 for two, on-site vans $20 for two.

Eating Out

Hideaway Restaurant, 22 Broad Street, ©4943 1431; *Jake Garden*, 9c Broad Street, ©4956 2221; and *Palms Restaurant*, The Esplanade, Sarina Beach, ©4956 6266.

POINTS OF INTEREST

Broad Street, the main street of the town, is indeed broad with a median strip in the centre offering tables, park benches and public amenities, and best of all, shade.

There are plenty of sandy beaches and offshore islands to entice you to swim, jog, fish or go boating.

The **Dalrymple Bay Coal Exporting Facilities** at Hay Point, ©4943 8444, are the largest of their type in the Southern Hemisphere.

CAPRICORN COAST

LOCATION AND CHARACTERISTICS

The Capricorn Coast stretches some 48km (30 miles) from Yeppoon and the Byfield area in the north to Keppel Sands in the south. The area enjoys a similar climate to that of Hawaii.

The main area of the Capricorn Coast begins at the town of Joskeleigh in the south and reaches north to the forests and national parks of Byfield. The primary town on the coast is Yeppoon, and the main city is Rockhampton, 41km inland. Rockhampton airport is the departure point for flights to the nearby islands of the Reef.

If you are swimming in the tropical waters of the Capricorn Coast, remember that deadly box jellyfish can be present in the sea anywhere north of the Tropic of Capricorn in the summer months.

VISITOR INFORMATION

The web page to visit online is ✆www.capricorncoast.com.au
Email for the Capricorn Coast Tourist Organisation is:
✉capcoast@cqnet.com.au

YEPPOON

Map H
Population 12,000

LOCATION AND CHARACTERISTICS

A modern town with a population of approximately 12,000, Yeppoon nestles beside pineapple-covered hills on the shores of Keppel Bay. Palms and pines line the main street, and shady trees continue to line the road to Rockhampton. There is a 4m difference between high and low tide, so trawlers, yachts and dinghies are left high and dry.

Yeppoon is the main town on the Capricorn Coast and is one of the largest and fastest growing coastal communities in Queensland. It is a popular holiday spot, offering access to more than 40km of safe beaches.

HOW TO GET THERE

By Coach

Young's Bus Service runs between Rockhampton and Yeppoon, ✆4922 3183 (Rockhampton) or ✆4939 3131 (Yeppoon).

By Car

If you have your own transport, the turn-off from the Bruce Highway for Yeppoon is just north of Rockhampton, and from there it is 40km (25 miles) towards the coast.

VISITOR INFORMATION

The Capricorn Coast Tourist Organisation has an office at the roundabout as you drive into town (you can't miss it!) and it is ⏱open daily 9am-5pm, ✆4939 4888.

ACCOMMODATION AND SERVICES

Here is a selection of available accommodation, with prices for a double room per night, which should be used as a guide only. The telephone area code is 07.

Capricorn International Resort, Farnborough Road, ✆4939 5111 or ✆1800 075 902 (toll free). 266 rooms, licensed restaurant, cocktail bar, swimming pool, sauna, spa, gymnasium, tennis golf, mini golf, archery, bowls, catamaran sailing, horse riding, scuba diving, volleyball, wind surfing, Kids Kapers, Teen Club - suites ✪$295-325, hotel section $185, apartment section $245-315.

Bayview Tower Motel, cnr Adelaide & Normanby Streets, ✆4939 4500. 34 units, licensed restaurant, swimming pool, spa, sauna - ✪$68-96.

Blue Anchor, 76 Whitman Street, ✆4939 4288. 8 units, barbecue, playground, undercover parking, heated pool - ✪$55-70.

Driftwood, 7 Todd Avenue, ✆4939 2446. 9 units, undercover parking, pool - ✪$55-69.

Strand Hotel/Motel, cnr Normanby Street & Anzac Parade, ✆4939 1301. 13 units, undercover parking, swimming pool - ✪$49.

Sail Inn Motel, 19 James Street, ✆4939 1130. 9 units, cooking facilities, barbecue, undercover parking - ✪$48-65.

Tidewater, 7 Normanby Street, ✆4939 1632. 8 flats, cooking facilities, undercover parking, heated pool - ✪$48-55.

Caravan Parks

Poinciana Tourist Park, 9 Scenic Highway, ✆4939 1601. 60 sites, barbecue, recreation room - powered sites ✪$15 for two, cabins $30-36 for two.

Beachside Caravan Park, Farnborough Road, ✆4939 3738. (No pets allowed) 70 sites, barbecue - powered sites ✪$14 for two.

Blue Dolphin Caravan Park, 74 Whitman Street, ☎4939 3140. (Pets on application) 47 sites - powered sites ✪$14 for two, cabins $30-33 for two.

Eating Out

You can select from the following.

Happy Sun Chinese Restaurant, 34 James Street, ☎ 4939 3323. Open daily with a smorgasbord dine-in on Sunday.

Footlights Theatre Restaurant, 123 Old Rockhampton Road, ☎4939 2399. Fully licensed with great food and entertainment.

Yeppoon Galaxy, Shop 4, 26 James Street, ☎4939 1205. Chinese restaurant open daily.

Beaches, Rosslyn Bay Harbour, ☎4933 6300. Open daily 7am until late with live entertainment Wed to Sun, including Sunday lunch.

Local Transport

Capricorn Cabs can be contacted on ☎4939 1999.

POINTS OF INTEREST

Cooberrie Park, 15km (9 miles) north of Yeppoon on Woodbury Road, is a bird and animal sanctuary with barbecue and picnic facilities. If you want to pat a kangaroo, this is the place to do it. They also have koalas and other native animals wandering freely through the parkland. It is ⏰open daily 9am-4.30pm and costs adults ✪$9 and children $4.50, ☎4939 7590.

Byfield State Forest Parks are 17km (10 miles) north of Cooberrie Park, and are popular picnic areas. They include Stoney Creek, Waterpark Creek and Red Rock Forest Parks.

Nob Creek Pottery, ☎4935 1161, established in 1979, is located in the tropical Byfield Forest, and has gained a reputation as a quality cottage industry.

Wreck Point at Cooee Bay provides a spectacular view overlooking the Keppel group of islands. It is situated on the southern outskirts of Yeppoon.

Rockhampton

Rosslyn Bay Boat Harbour is the base for a large fishing fleet, charter boats, *Keppel Isles Yacht Charters* (12 Poplar Street, Yeppoon, ℭ4939 4949), cruise boats and catamarans. Cruises available include coral viewing, boom netting and, weather permitting, a visit to Middle Island Underwater Observatory.

Emu Park, 19km (12 miles) south of Yeppoon and linked by the Capricorn Coast Scenic Highway, has an unusual memorial to Captain Cook - a singing ship. The mast, sail and rigging contain hollow pipes, and the ship 'sings' when the wind blows. This picturesque town is worth the short and scenic drive for a visit.

Capricorn Coast Tours are located at 50 McBean Street, Yeppoon, ℭ4349 1325.

GREAT KEPPEL ISLAND

Map H

LOCATION AND CHARACTERISTICS

The island is a very popular tourist destination. Fringed by 17km (10 miles) of white, sandy beaches and offshore coral reefs, it provides an ideal setting for holiday makers and day trippers alike.

The Keppel Island group of 30 islands is situated 55km from Rockhampton, and 15km east of Rosslyn Bay on the Capricorn Coast. Great Keppel is the only island in the group to have been developed, and this is because of its permanent water supply as well as its size (14 sq km).

Some islands in the group are national parks - North Keppel, Miall, Middle, Halfway, Humpy and Peak - where camping is permitted, but numbers are limited. All drinking water has to be taken to these islands, but some have water for washing, and some have toilets, but it is best to get full information from either the Naturally Queensland Information Centre in Brisbane, ℭ3227 8187, or the QNP&WS branch on the corner of Yeppoon & Norman Roads, Rockhampton, ℰ4936 0511, when applying for a camping permit. It is also wise to check on the fishing regulations for the area you are going to visit.

Great Keppel

In May 1770 Captain Cook sailed past Great Keppel and named it after Admiral Augustus Keppel, who later became the First Lord of the Admiralty.

A naturalist from the *Rattlesnake* is given the credit of being the first European to visit the island when he came ashore in 1847, but the Woppabura Aboriginal people had been living there for over 4,500 years. They called the island Wapparaburra.

The first European settlers arrived in 1906, but they could not live happily with the Aborigines and in fact treated them very badly. The Leeke family moved to the island in the 1920s and grazed sheep there until the 1940s. Their name is remembered in Leeke's Beach and Leeke's Creek, and the restored Homestead is where they lived. The resort opened in 1967.

Although not situated on the Reef, Great Keppel is the gateway to the Outer Reef and North West Island, the largest coral cay in the Great Barrier Reef. It is a major breeding ground for Green Turtles, White Capped Noddy Terns, Wedge Tailed Shearwaters and Olive Head Sea Snakes.

Day trips to Great Keppel Island are available from *Keppel Tourist Services*, ℰ4933 6744 or ℰ1800 356 744 (free call). The trip lasts 8 hours and includes a cruise transfer from Rosslyn Bay, snorkelling and boom netting, buffet lunch and free time. The day trip costs ✪$70 adults, $40 children and $180 for families.

HOW TO GET THERE

By Air

15 minute air transfers are available from Rockhampton Airport, ℰ4936 8314 for more details. There are also coach transfers from the airport to Rosslyn Bay.

Rockhampton

By Coach

If you are staying in Rockhampton, contact Rothery's Coaches, ✆4922 4320, or Young's Bus Service, ✆4922 3813, to check times for connecting bus services to Rosslyn Bay. The coach trip usually costs around ✪$24 for an adult.

By Sea

Ferries leave from Rosslyn Bay Harbour, south of Yeppoon.

Keppel Tourist Services, ✆4933 6744.

Capricornia Cruises, ✆4933 6730.

Australis Cruises, ✆0418 728 965.

Euphoria Catamaran Cruises, ✆1300 301 251

You can expect to pay upwards of ✪$70 for a family of four.

By Car

Visitors that have their own transport can enquire about long-term parking at Kempsea Car Park, 422 Scenic Highway, Rosslyn Harbour, ✆4933 6670, which is north of the harbour turn-off, on the main road, and has complimentary transport from there to the wharf.

VISITOR INFORMATION

If you would like online details of the Great Keppel Island Resort, the web site is 👁www.mpx.com.au/~adventures/gk/keppel.htm

ACCOMMODATION AND SERVICES

The *Great Keppel Island Resort*, ✆4939 5044, has over 190 units, labelled Garden, Beachfront or Hillside Villas. The Garden and Beachfront are rated 3-star, and the Villas are 4-star.

Resort facilities are: nightclub, live entertainment, 2 restaurants, bars, heated swimming pool, spa, kids' club, games room, squash, tennis courts, laundry/ironing, quick snack bar, fishing, babysitting, tube rides, golf, tandem-skydiving, cricket, waterskiing, parasailing, baseball, snorkelling, sailboarding, catamaran sailing, beach volleyball, SCUBA diving, cruising and coral-viewing, Barrier Reef trips and EFTPOS.

Rockhampton

Unit facilities are: tea and coffee making facilities, refrigerator, ceiling fans (Garden and Beachfront) air-conditioning (Ocean View), colour TV, in-house movies, IDD/STD telephone, radio, inter-connecting rooms and a daily cleaning service.

Tariffs for a double room per night night are:

Garden -   ✪$154-280 adult
Beachfront -   ✪$176-350 adult
Hillside Villas - ✪$218-398 adult

The above rates are room only. Cheaper rates are available for longer stays, and packages are available which include meals.

Additional to the tariffs are: Barrier Reef trips, boom netting, cruising and coral viewing, deserted island drop-off, dinghies with outboards, fishing and yacht charters, island waterways cruise, kids camp-out (children 5-14 years), masseuse, scuba diving courses, scuba diving trips to the Great Barrier Reef, sunset cruise, tandem skydiving, tube rides, underwater observatory and waterskiing.

Reservations can be made by contacting the resort directly on ©4939 5044. Credit cards accepted: Visa, MasterCard, Bankcard, Diners Club, American Express.

Keppel Haven, ©4933 6744, have 12 cabins with cooking facilities, but bathrooms and laundry are shared. The room-only tariff is ✪$110 per night for a double.

Resort facilities include kiosk, gift shop, licensed restaurant, dive shop, jet ski and water sports hire.

There are also pre-erected tents that cost ✪$22 per person, in the Breeze Way section. There is undercover communal cooking and washing up, a refreigerator and barbecue, but no kitchen utensils.

And lastly, there is the Tent Village, where you must provide your own bedding and linen, and use common cooking facilities. There are units here for ✪$25 a night per person.

The **Great Keppel YHA Hostel**, ©4927 5288, is a self-contained area within the Keppel Haven complex. It has 20 rooms in the main

building, with a kitchen, bathrooms and a laundry. Tariffs are ✪$18 per adult twin share. Bookings and courtesy transfer arrangements can be made direct or through Rockhampton ΥΗΑ, ✆4927 5288.

Local Transport

There are no motor vehicles on the island, so you can walk the many bush tracks or relax on the beach in peace.

Sailing on the Great Barrier Reef

Rockhampton

Eating Out

Apart from the restaurants at the accommodation complexes, there are a couple of additional choices:

Between the Resort and Keppel Haven is the **Shell House**, ✆4939 1004, where you can get really tasty Devonshire tea, or pick up some scones and cakes for afternoon tea back at the tent or cabin. The place has, of course, a good shell collection, and contains information on the history of the island.

Nearby on The Esplanade is **Island Pizza**, ✆4939 4699, which also sells hot dogs, subs and pasta, all at reasonable prices.

POINTS OF INTEREST

The **Middle Island Underwater Observatory** is a popular attraction. It is surrounded by natural coral, and the area teems with marine life of every type imaginable. A sunken wreck nearby also provides a haven for fish, sea snakes, turtles and a school of huge cod.

The Underwater Observatory is ⏱open daily 8am-5pm, if weather conditions are favourable, and admission charges are ✪$10 adults and $5 children.

There are ample opportunities for fishing, cruising, boom netting, windsurfing and bushwalking.

DIVING

A glance at a map will show that the Great Barrier Reef is a long way from the mainland at this point, but there is some good diving closer to Great Keppel Island. Bald Rock and Man & Wife Rocks are popular diving venues, and between the southern end of Halfway Island and Middle Island Reef there is some good coral.

If the weather is calm there is good diving at Parker's Bombora, off the south-eastern tip of Great Keppel. It begins in water about 20m deep and is encircled by sea ferns, sponges, coral and hundreds of fish.

The outer islands of the Keppel group, particularly Barren Island, have deeper and clearer water than Great Keppel, so larger species of sea life are encountered, like turtles and manta rays.

All diving gear can be hired from the accommodation outlets on Great Keppel.

HERON ISLAND

Map A

LOCATION AND CHARACTERISTICS

The island is about 72km east of Gladstone, roughly 100km from Rockhampton, and has an area of 19ha. It is a true coral cay that sits on the Tropic of Capricorn, surrounded by 24 sq km of reef.

It is possible to walk around the island in less than half an hour, and there is usually an organised beach and reef walk every day. Heron's eastern end has a track system that leads through dense pisonia forest and open grassy shrubland, with information posts along the way. In the summer months be sure to stay on the track, or you could destroy one of the many shearwater burrows that honeycomb the island.

Rockhampton

The survey vessel *Fly* was the first to record the existence of Heron Island during its voyage of 1843. The captain named the island after the many reef herons, which are now known as reef egrets. Nothing much is recorded about visitors to the islands until around 1910 when bird-watchers and other naturalists came to explore. These groups did not usually have their bases on Heron, so their visits were only brief sojourns.

In the mid-1920s a canning factory was built where the resort office now stands, and turtle harvesting began. By the end of the decade the supply of turtles had dwindled and industry here ceased, although some turtles were caught here and sent south right up until they were declared a protected species in 1950. The clumsy creatures still come to Heron to lay their eggs.

In 1932, the canning factory was converted into a resort by Cristian Poulsen, and in 1936 he was granted the special lease on which the resort is built. Many facilities were added to the resort, and a regular flying-boat service was established before Poulsen disappeared from a dinghy near the island in 1947. The resort remained in the family until 1974.

The Heron Island research station commenced operations in 1951 and has an international reputation for coral reef research and education. In 1943 a national park was declared on Heron Island, and in 1974 Queensland's first marine National Park was declared over the Heron and Wistari Reefs. In 1979 the Capricornia section of the Great Barrier Reef Marine Park was declared under new federal government legislation.

HOW TO GET THERE

Unfortunately, due to its distance from the mainland, Heron Island is one of the most expensive islands to visit.

By Air

Marine Helicopters, at Gladstone Airport, ©4978 1177, fly from Gladstone to Heron Island on a 30 minute trip. They don't have a

Rockhampton

regular schedule, but will meet flights into Gladstone to transfer passengers to the island. Obviously it is best to contact them before you arrive in Gladstone. Fares for adults are ✪$240 one-way, $395 return, half-price for children.

By Sea

A catamaran makes the trip from Gladstone to Heron in a little under two hours, but it can be a very choppy trip, so make sure you have some seasickness pills. It departs at 11am and returns about 3.45pm. Fares are ✪$75 each way (adult), $37.50 each way for children. Bookings can be made through the Resort.

VISITOR INFORMATION

There is a website at ☞www.heronisland.com and email at ✉visitors@greatberrierreef.aus.net

The Resort can be phoned direct on ✆132 469.

ACCOMMODATION

The **Heron Island Resort**, ✆4978 1488 or ✆132 469, has 5 types of accommodation - 30 Turtle Cabins, 44 Reef Suites, 38 Heron Suites, 1 Beach House and 4 Point Suites.

> The Cabins are budget bungalows, with basic facilities, shared bathroom and bunk sleeping arrangements. You may find yourself housed with strangers to make up numbers.

The Suites have a balcony and ensuite, and accommodate up to four people. The Point Suites are an extra-large version.

The Beach House occupies a premium beachfront position and has a balcony and ensuite. It accommodates two adults only.

Tarrifs per person per night are as follows:

Turtle Cabins -   ✪$170 adults, $85 children.

Reef Suites -   ✪$245 (adults, twin share), $123 children.

Heron Suites -   ✪$278 (adults, twin share), $139 children.

Beach House -   ✪$435.

Point Suites -   ✪$360 (adults, twin share), $180 children.

These prices include all meals, and most activities.

YEPPOON-ROCKHAMPTON

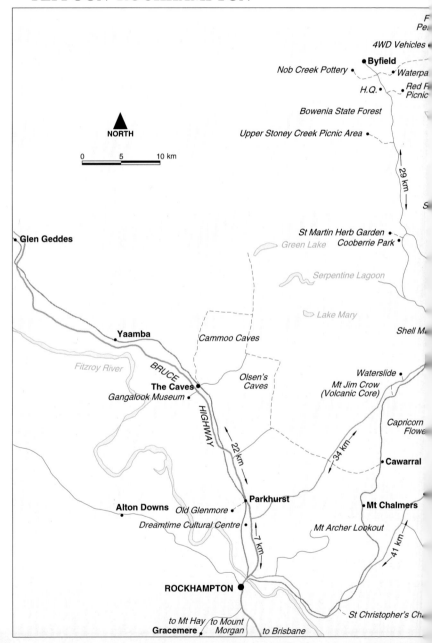

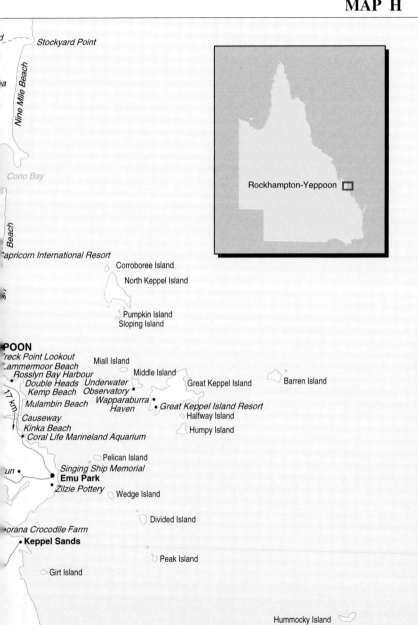

ROCKHAMPTON

MAP I

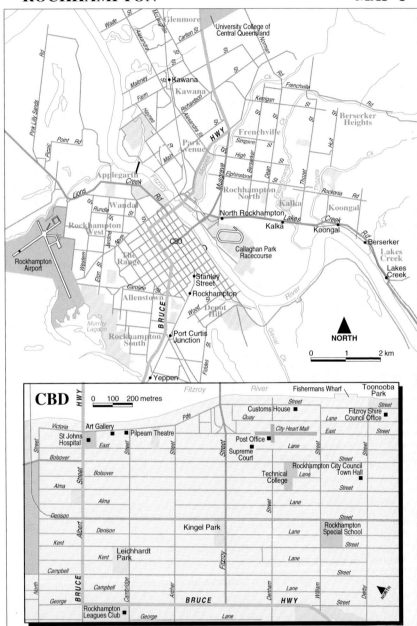

Resort facilities are: restaurant, cocktail bar, coffee shop, tennis court, games room, two swimming pools, babysitting, discotheque, entertainment, reef walks, jumbo outdoor chess, dive shop, resort shop, SCUBA courses, snorkelling, Kids' Klub during school holiday and a semi-submersible reef viewer.

Rooms have private facilities, tea and coffee making facilities, refrigerator, mini bar on request, ceiling fans, daily cleaning service and inter-connecting rooms.

Credit cards accepted: Visa, MasterCard, Bankcard, American Express.

DIVING

At other islands on the Reef it is sometimes necessary to travel 70 or 80 km for scuba diving and snorkelling, but at Heron the Reef is at the very foot of the white sandy beaches.

One of the most spectacular diving sites is the well-known Heron Bommie, a head of hard coral rising more than 18m from the seabed that is home to all kinds of fish and marine life.

All equipment can be hired from the resort's dive shop, and the six-day certificate diving course costs around ✪$400. Day dives, including all equipment, cost around $50.

Heron hosts a week-long Dive Festival in November each year, when divers from all over the world gather to swap knowledge and experience. There are those who think that this island rates highly among the world's premier dive locations, and given that there are twenty unique sites nearby, they are probably right.

LADY MUSGRAVE ISLAND

Map A

LOCATION AND CHARACTERISTICS

Lady Musgrave Island is part of the Capricorn Bunker Group, and is about 100km north-east of Bundaberg. It is a true coral cay, approximately 18ha in area, and rests on the edge of a huge coral lagoon that measures some eight kilometres in circumference and covers an area of around 1192ha. The lagoon is one of very few on the Reef that ships can enter, making the island very popular with the yachting fraternity. Lady Musgrave is a National and Marine Park, and an unspoilt section of the Great Barrier Reef.

HOW TO GET THERE

MV *Lady Musgrave* is a catamaran that sails from Port Bundaberg on Tues, Thurs, Sat and Sun, with extra services during school holidays. Even so, it is always advisable to book well ahead through Lady Musgrave Barrier Reef Cruises, Bundaberg Port Marina, Shop 1 Moffatt Street, Bundaberg, ✆4159 4519 or ✆1800 072 110. The trip out to the island takes about two-and-a-half hours, and passengers are allowed four hours on the island.

On reaching the island passengers are transferred to the semi-submersible for some coral viewing, and on returning to the catamaran a visit is made to the underwater observatory. Lunch is then served and afterwards passengers are taken ashore to explore the island. Snorkelling gear is provided for the day.

The cruise costs are ✪$165 for one certified dive, $185 for two dives, $175 for a diving introduction and $115 for snorkelling.

This cruise can also be used for people wishing to camp on Lady Musgrave.

ACCOMMODATION

There is no choice in this regard - if you wish to stay on Lady Musgrave Island you must camp. There are staff on-site, toilets and walking trails, and that is it. You have to first obtain a camping permit from the QNP&WS or Naturally Queensland, ✆3227 8187, and fees are ✪$3.50 per person per night.

DIVING

The island is reputedly one of the finest dive sites on the Great Barrier Reef, and is home to around 1200 species of fish and 350 varieties of coral. The lagoon is reasonably shallow, allowing longer dives to be undertaken.

MV *Lady Musgrave* always has qualified diving instructors on board for the inexperienced, but they can also head certified divers in the best direction to get the most out of their trip.

LADY ELLIOT ISLAND

Map A

LOCATION AND CHARACTERISTICS

The most southerly of the islands of the Great Barrier Reef, Lady Elliot has an area of 0.42 sq km and has been nicknamed Queensland's "Shipwreck Island". This name is not unwarranted, as the wrecks of many ships can be seen littered around the island's shores. The first was probably in 1851, the *Bolton Abbey* cargo ship, and the latest was the *Tenggara II* which hit the reef in April, 1989.

The island is also popular with bird watchers as 57 species are known to flock here, with more than 200,000 birds nesting here during the summer. Sea turtles also nest on Lady Elliot.

HOW TO GET THERE

By Air

The island has an airstrip serviced by Whitaker Air Charters, ✆1800 072 200 (free call), whose scenic flights operate daily from both Bundaberg and Hervey Bay.

These flights can be taken by resort guests, or by day-trippers for whom the fare includes the return flight, a picnic lunch, reef walking and snorkelling.

VISITOR INFORMATION

Contact the resort on ✆3348 8522 or ✆1800 072 200 (free call). You can visit the web page at ✆www.ladyelliot.com.au or send an email to ✉info@ladyelliot.com.au

Rockhampton

ACCOMMODATION

The **Lady Elliot Island Resort**, ℰ1800 072 200, is located on the beach front, and is rated at 2-star. There are 5 Island Suites, 24 Reef Units, 14 Tent Cabins and 6 Lodges.

The Resort has a licensed restaurant, cocktail bar, swimming pool, entertainment, novelty golf course, dive shop, resort shop, poolside bar and bistro, Reef Education Centre, glass bottom boat, baby sitting, snorkelling, scuba courses, guided eco tours, charter fishing boat, and a tour desk.

Units have private facilities, fans, balcony and maid service.

Prices per person per night, twin share, are:

Island Suite -　　❂$198 adults, $99 children

Reef Cabin -　　　❂$176, $88 children

Tent or Lodge -　❂$137 adults, $69 children

Tariff includes accommodation, dinner, breakfast and snorkelling equipment.

Maximum occupancy of each unit is 4 persons (including children). Credit cards accepted: Visa, MasterCard, Bankcard, American Express, Diners Club.

POINTS OF INTEREST

It only takes about an hour to walk around the entire island, and it is one of the least commercialised.

DIVING

There are ten excellent diving sites that include Lighthouse Bommie, Coral Gardens, Moiri and Shark Pool. Visibility ranges from 80 to 25 to 50 metres. This island is also paradise for those who like exploring shipwrecks.

All equipment can be hired from the resort for around $50, and open water courses are available for ❂$484. Shore dives cost $27.50, boat dives $38.50 and night dives $49.50.

ROCKHAMPTON

Map I
Population 65,000
Gateway to the Capricorn Coast, Rockhampton is 660km (410 miles) north of Brisbane, on the Tropic of Capricorn. The city is situated on the Fitzroy River about 16km (10 miles) from the coast.

CLIMATE

Average temperatures: January max 31C (88F) - min 22C (72F); July max 23C (73F) - min 9C (48F). Most rain falls between December and March - approximately 500mm (17 in).

CHARACTERISTICS

'Rocky' is the heart of the beef cattle country. The main breeds are Santa Gertrudis, Hereford, Braford, Brahman, Africander and Zebu. Rockhampton also has two flour mills which process wheat from the Central Highlands around Emerald. Ever since Queensland became a separate state, there have been people politicising for the establishment of a separate North Queensland state.

HOW TO GET THERE

By Air

Ansett, ✆13 1300, fly to/from Brisbane, Mackay, Melbourne and Sydney.
Sunstate, ✆13 1313, fly to/from Bundaberg, Gladstone, Mackay, Maryborough, Townsville and Cairns, Great Keppel Island and Toowoomba.
Eastern Airlines, ✆13 1313, fly to/from the Gold Coast.

By Bus

Greyhound Pioneer, ✆13 2030, and McCaffertys, ✆13 1499, stop at Rockhampton on their Brisbane/North Queensland route.
McCaffertys have a daily service to/from Longreach.
Greyhound also have a Rockhampton/Longreach service departing 3 times weekly.

Rockhampton

By Rail

Queensland Tilt Trains, ✆13 2235, including The Spirit of Capricorn, service Rockhampton fairly frequently, with either day or overnight travel. The Sunlander and the Queenslander both leave Brisbane in the early morning and stop at Rockhampton.

By Car

From Brisbane, via the Bruce Highway 660km (410 miles), or take the inland route via Esk and Biloela 758km (470 miles). Rockhampton is 1413km (878 miles) south of Cairns.

VISITOR INFORMATION

Capricorn Tourism Inc., is at 'The Spire' in Gladstone Road, ✆4927 2055, adjacent to the Tropic of Capricorn Spire. It is ⏰open 7 days a week.

The email address is ✎captour@rocknet.net.au and the website is ☞www.capricorncoast.com.au

You will find the Rockhampton Tourist Information Centre in Quay Street, ✆4922 5339.

ACCOMMODATION

Rockhampton has no shortage of motels, and there are plenty of older style hotels near the city centre. There is also no shortage of camping grounds. Below we have given a selection with prices for a double room per night, which should be used as a guide only. The telephone area code is 07.

Country Comfort Rockhampton, 86 Victoria Parade, ✆4927 9933. 78 units, licensed restaurant, barbecue, swimming pool - ✪$102.

Ambassador on the Park, 161 George Street, ✆4927 5855. 70 units, 3 suites, licensed restaurant, swimming pool - ✪$70-110.

Archer Park, 39 Albert Street, ✆4927 9266. 26 units, licensed restaurant, swimming pool, undercover parking - ✪$70-75.

Sundowner Chain Motor Inns Rockhampton, 112 Gladstone Road, ✆4927 8866. 32 units, licensed restaurant, swimming pool - ✪$69-80.

Central Park, 224 Murray Street, ✆4927 2333. 26 units, licensed restaurant (closed Sun), swimming pool - ✪$49-59.

Leichardt Hotel Rockhampton, cnr Bolsover & Denham Streets, ✆4927 6733. 60 rooms, 8 suites, licensed restaurant and bistro - ✪$95-110.

Club Crocodile Motor Inn, cnr Albert & Alma Streets, ✆4927 7433. 44 units, licensed restaurant (closed Sunday), swimming pool - ✪$78-95.

Glenmore Palms, Bruce Highway, Glenmore, North Rockhampton, ✆4926 1144. 38 units, licensed restaurant, swimming pool, spa - ✪$81-86.

Centre Point Motor Inn, 131 George Street, ✆4927 8844. 48 units, licensed restaurant, heated swimming pool - ✪$82.

Golden Fountain Motel, 166 Gladstone Road, ✆4927 1055. 31 units, swimming pool - ✪$50-80.

Caravan Parks

Big 4 Tropical Wanderer Holiday Village, 394 Yaamba Road, ✆4926 3822. (No pets) 150 sites, licensed restaurants, barbecue, tennis (half court), pool - powered sites ✪$19 for two, cabins $41-50 for two.

Ramblers Motor Village, Bruce Highway, North Rockhampton, (opposite Shopping Fair), ✆4928 2084. (No pets) 60 sites, playground, pool - powered sites ✪$17 for two, units $47-51 for two, cabins $37-43 for two.

Southside Holiday Village, Lower Dawson Road, ✆4927 3013. 200 sites, heated pool, tennis (half court) - powered sites ✪$16-18 for two, on-site vans $31 for two, cabins 40-47 for two.

Municipal Riverside Caravan Park, Reaney Street, North Rockhampton, ✆4922 3779. (No pets allowed) 150 sites - powered sites ✪$13.50 for two.

Gracemere Caravan Park, Old Capricorn Highway, ✆4933 1310. 100 sites, barbecue, pool - powered sites ✪$11.

There is a **Youth Hostel** at 60 McFarlane Street, North Rockhampton, ✆4927 5288. They have 13 rooms at ✪$18 per adult per night twin share.

Rockhampton

EATING OUT

Most of the hotels serve casual counter meals, and the steaks in Rocky are particularly large, as this is the heart of the cattle country. The hotels, and several motels, also have licensed restaurants. A wide assortment of cuisine is available, from Chinese to seafood. Here are some names and numbers of establishments in the area:

Dragon Gallery, 295 Richardson Road, North Rockhampton, ✆4928 3399. Traditional Chinese cuisine.

Hogs Breath Cafe, Aquatic Place, North Rockhampton, ✆4926 3646. Hamburgers and steaks.

Hong Kong Seafood Restaurant, 98a Denham Street, Rockhampton, ✆4927 7144.

Pacinos, cnr Fitzroy & George Streets, Rockhampton, ✆4922 5833. Italian fare.

Thai Tanee Restaurant, cnr Bolsover & William Streets, Rockhampton, ✆4922 1255.

Wah Hah, 70 Denham Street, Rockhampton, ✆4927 1659. Chinese selections.

Sizzler, Rockhamtpon Shopping Fair, Rockhampton, ✆4926 1100. Australian steaks and salad.

Cravings Bar and Grill, cnr Water Street and Lakes Creek Road, North Rockhampton, ✆4928 5666.

Le Bistro on Quay, 194 Quay Street, Rockhampton, ✆4922 2019.

Cactus Jacks Restaurant, 243 Musgrave Street, North Rockhampton, ✆4922 2062.

Diamonds Down by the River, Quay Street, Rockhampton, ✆4921 1811.

Friends Bistro, 159 East Street, Rockhampton, ✆4922 2689.

Jans Restaurant, Pilbeam Theatre, Victoria Parade, Rockhampton, ✆4922 3060.

There are two McDonalds branches, one on the Bruce Highway in North Rockhampton and the other on the corner of George and Fitzroy Streets, Rockhampton. KFC also has two outlets, one at the corner of George and Arthur Streets, Rockhampton, and the other on the corner of Linnet Street and Queen Elizabeth Drive, North Rockhampton. Pizza Hut is on the corner of High Street and Bruce Highway, North Rochampton, and on the corner of Denham Street and Bruce Highway in Rockhampton, ℓ13 1166.

ENTERTAINMENT

Rockhampton has a three cinema complex in Shopping Fair, North Rockhampton, ℓ4926 6977, and indoor and outdoor concert venues.

There are three nightclubs in the city:

Strutters, cnr East & Williams Streets, ℓ4922 2882.

The Party Shack, cnr William & Alma Streets, ℓ4927 2005.

William Street Nite Club, 4 William Street, ℓ4927 1144.

The *Pilbeam Theatre* in Victoria Parade attracts regular performances by national and international artists, ℓ4927 4111.

For details of current entertainment programs at hotels, clubs, and so on, ask at the Visitor Information Centre.

SHOPPING

Rockhampton has never been described as a shopping capital, but the *Shopping Fair*, Yaaamba Road, North Rockhampton, ℓ4928 9166, was refurbished a few years ago and should cater to your basic needs. It has a departent store, two supermarkets, over 100 specialty shops, a food court, and a licensed restaurant.

The *City Heart Mall*, in Bolsover Street, has local art and craft markets on Saturdays, ℓ4936 8481.

POINTS OF INTEREST

Rockhampton was first settled in the 1850s by Charles and William Archer. Today, historic **Quay Street** contains over 20 buildings which have been classified by the National Trust.

The city is the commercial and administrative centre of central Queensland. Its wide streets are lined with trees and solid buildings, indicating a prosperity dating back to the early days. The Australian Estate Co Ltd offices were built in 1861, and the Customs House in 1901.

Rockhampton

It has a handsome copper dome and a striking semi-circular portico. Queens Wharf is all that remains of the quays of the port that was very busy until silt caused the demise of the river trade. St Joseph's Cathedral (cnr Murray and William Streets) and St Paul's Anglican Cathedral are both built in Gothic Style from local sandstone. The Royal Arcade was built in 1889 as a theatre with a special feature - the roof could be opened on hot nights.

The Botanic Gardens in Spencer Street, ✆4922 4347, are reputed to be one of the finest tropical gardens in Australia. Spreading over 4ha (10 acres), these gardens contain many native and exotic trees, ferns and shrubs, as well as a large walk-in aviary, orchid and fern house and a small Australian Zoo, which includes its own Koala Park. As part of a sister city agreement with Ibusuki City in Japan, separate Japanese Gardens were created in 1982. There are also paddle boat rides available on the lagoon. The gardens are ⊙open 6am-6pm daily and admission is free.

The Pilbeam Theatre, ✆4927 4111 and **Art Gallery**, ✆4936 8248, in Victoria Parade, form the cultural centre of Rocky. The Art Gallery has an extensive collection of Australian paintings, pottery and sculpture. The Pilbeam Theatre attracts regular performances by national and international stars.

St Aubin's Village, on Canoona Road beside the airport, consists of one of Rockhampton's oldest houses, and a number of gift shops specialising in cottage industries. It is ⊙open 9am-6pm Mon-Sat and on Sundays 9am-2pm. Admission is free.

Callaghan Park Racecourse, ✆4927 1300, is Queensland's premier provincial racetrack. Thursday night has greyhound racing, Saturday evening has harness racing, and on Saturday afternoon it's the gallopers' turn.

Fitzroy River Ski Gardens, near the Barrage bridge, beside the boat launching facilities, has picnic facilities, a children's playground and electric barbecues.

Old Glenmore Homestead, ✆4936 1033, through the Parkhurst Industrial Estate in the north of the city, is a 130-year-old complex consisting of a log cabin, slab cottage and an adobe house. Old Glenmore holds Queensland's first Historic Inn Licence, so visitors can sample some of the State's best fermented beverages in this pleasant old world setting. Bush dances and home-style cooking are also features. It is ◷open only on Sundays between 11am and 3pm. Admission is ✪$6 for adults and $1.50 for children. Groups are allowed by appointment.

Cammoo Caves, ✆4934 2774, and **Olsen's Capricorn Caverns**, ✆4934 2883, approximately 23km (14miles) north of Rockhampton, are two cave systems which are open to the public. Cave coral, fossils and gigantic tree roots can be inspected in these dry, limestone caves. Cammoo Caves are ◷open daily 8.30am-4.30pm and have conducted tours. Entry fees are adults ✪$7 and children $3. Olsen's, about 2km east of Cammoo, is privately owned, and 3 hour half-day tours into these caves cost ✪$28 adults, $14 children, departing from your accommodation in Rockhampton around 9am.

The Dreamtime Cultural Centre, ✆4936 1655, is a large Aboriginal Cultural Centre, and is on the Bruce Highway opposite the turn-off to Yeppoon. The centre is ◷open daily 10am-5.15pm, with guided tours between 11am and 4pm (2 hours duration). Refreshments are available (eating bush tucker is not compulsory). Adults are charged ✪$11 and children $5.

Rockhampton Heritage Village is in Boundary Road, Parkhurst, ✆4936 1026. Attractions include a blacksmith's shop, wheel

Rockhampton

wrighting, dairy, fully furnished slab cottage, pioneering tools, vintage cars, horse-drawn vehicles, Hall of Clocks and a kiosk. Tours are conducted daily, and there are working demonstrations on the last Sunday of each month. It is ⊕open daily 10am-4pm and admission is ✪$9.50 adults and $5.50 children.

Koorana Crocodile Farm is in Koowonga Road, off Emu Park Road. This is a breeding farm, not a protective reserve, so don't be surprised when when you find crocodile kebabs on the menu, and crocodile skin shoes and purses for sale in the gift shop. The Crocodile Farm is ⊕open daily and costs adults ✪$13.30, children $6.60, and $9.90 per person for groups.

SPORT

Rockhampton has all the usual facilities you would expect of a town of its size. To get to the beach, though, you have to drive 45km to the Capricorn Coast.

DIVING

Capricorn Reef Diving, 189 Musgrave Street, North Rockhampton, ✆4922 7720, offer 5-day open water certificate PADI course. Classes are taken in Rockhampton, followed by 4 dives on the Keppel Island Group.

TOURS

Rothery's Coaches, 13 Power Street, North Rockhampton, ✆4922 4320, offer tours of the city and to the Capricorn Coast, Koorana Crocodile Farm, Cooberrie Park, The Caves and the Dreamtime Culture Centre. *Duncan's Off Road 4WD Tours* are in Kent Street, Rockhampton, ✆0418 986 050 (mobile).

PART THREE

Appendix

INTERNET INFORMATION

INTERNATIONAL AIRLINES

Air New Zealand
👁www.airnz.com.au
✏email service under *Contact Us*
then *Online Booking Enquiries*
☎13 24 76

Ansett
👁www.ansett.com.au
✏email service under *About Ansett*
then *Contacts*
☎13 13 00

British Airways
👁www.british-airways.com
☎8904 8800

Canadian Airlines
👁www.cdnair.ca
✏comments@cdnair.ca
☎1300 655 767

Cathay Pacific
👁www.cathaypacific.com/australia
✏email service under *Feedback*
☎13 17 47

Qantas
👁www.qantas.com.au
✏email service under *Contacts* then
Enquiries and Feedback
☎13 13 13

Singapore Airlines
👁www.singaporeair.com.au
✏info_syd@singaporeair.com.au
☎13 10 11

United Airlines
👁www.unitedairlines.com
✏email service under *Contact
United*
☎13 17 77

DOMESTIC AIRLINES

Airlink
👁www.qantas.com.au/flights/
regional/airlink.html
☎13 13 13

Ansett
👁www.ansett.com.au
✉email service under *About Ansett*
then *Contacts*
☎13 13 00

Eastern Australia Airlines
👁www.qantas.com.au/flights/
regional/eastern.html
☎13 13 13

Flight West
👁www.flightwest.com.au
✉flightwest@fltwest.com.au
☎1300 130 092

Hazelton
👁www.hazelton.com.au
✉email service under *Customer Feedback*
☎13 17 13

Impulse Airlines
👁www.impulseairlines.com.au
☎13 13 81

Kendell
👁www.kendell.com.au
✉kendell@kendell.com.au
☎(03) 9670 2677

Qantas
👁www.qantas.com.au
✉email service under *Contacts* then
Enquiries and Feedback
☎13 13 13

Sunstate
👁www.qantas.com.au/flights/
regional/sunstate.html
☎13 13 13

Virgin Blue
👁www.virginblue.com.au
☎13 6789

INTER- AND INTRASTATE RAIL SERVICES

Countrylink
👁www.countrylink.nsw.gov.au
✉bookings@countrylink.nsw.gov.au
☎13 22 32

Great Southern Railway
👁www.gsr.com.au
✉salesagent@gsr.com.au
☎13 21 47

Queensland Rail Traveltrain
👁qroti.bit.net.au/traveltrain
✉qroti@proceed.com.au or
✉res.traveltrain@qr.com.au
☎13 2232

Rail Australia
👁www.railaustralia.com.au
✉info@railaustralia.com.au

INTERSTATE COACH SERVICES

Greyhound Pioneer
👁www.greyhound.com.au
✉express@greyhound.com.au
☎13 20 30

McCaffertys
👁www.mccaffertys.com.au
✉infomcc@mccaffertys.com.au
☎13 14 99

OVERSEAS VISITORS INFORMATION

Australian Tourist Commission
👁www.australia.com
✎email service under *Ask Us*
☎1300 361 650

Australian Quarantine
👁 www.aqis.gov.au
☎1800 020 504

Customs Australia
👁www.customs.gov.au
☎1300 363 263

Foreign Currency Exchange
👁www.xe.net/ucc

Telephone Numbers
👁www.whitepages.com.au
👁www.yellowpages.com.au
👁www.colourpages.com.au
☎1223

VISITOR INFORMATION - AUSTRALIA

Australian Tourist Commission
👁www.australia.com
✎email service under *Contact Us*
☎1300 361 650

VISITOR INFORMATION - QUEENSLAND

GENERAL
Environmental Protection Agency
👁www.env.qld.gov.au
☎(07) 3224 5641

Naturally Queensland
👁www.env.qld.gov.au/environment/feature/nqic
✎nqic@env.qld.gov.au
☎(07) 3227 8187

Queensland Government
👁www.qld.gov.au
☎1800 803 788

Queensland Holidays
👁www.queensland-holidays.com.au

Tourism Queensland
👁www.qttc.com.au
or 👁www.tq.com.au
✎qttcinfo@qttc.com.au
☎(07) 3406 5400

BRISBANE
Brisbane Local Coucil
👁www.brisbane.qld.gov.au

Brisbane Tourism
👁www.brisbanetourism.com.au
✎enquiries@brisbanetourism.com.au
☎(07) 3221 8411

Transinfo
👁www.transinfo.qld.gov.au
☎13 1230

REGIONAL
Airlie Tourist Information Centre
✎abtic@whitsunday.net.au
☎(07) 4946 6665

Bedarra Island Resort
👁www.bedarraisland.com
✎visitors@greatbarrierreef.aus.net
☎(07) 4068 8233

Brampton Island Resort

👁 www.bramptonislandresort.com

✆ 4951 4097

Cape York Tourist Info

👁 www.visitcapeyork.com

Capricorn Coast Tourist Organisation

👁 www.capricorncoast.com.au

✉ capcoast@cqnet.com.au

✆ (07) 4939 4888

Capricorn Tourism

👁 www.capricorncoast.com.au

✉ captour@rocknet.net.au

✆ (07) 4927 2055

Charters Towers Dalrymple Tourist Information Centre

✉ tourinfocentre@httech.com.au

✆ (07) 4752 0314

Club Crocodile Resort Long Island

👁 www.clubcrocodile.com.au

✆ (07) 4946 9233

Club Med Lindeman Island

👁 www.clubmed.com.au

✆ (07) 4946 9633

Cooktown Tourism Association

👁 www.cooktownau.com

✉ info@cooktownau.com

✆ 1800 001 770

Daintree Tourist Information

👁 www.greatbarrierreef.aus.net

or 👁 www.tnq.org.au

✆ (07) 4098 6120

Daydream Island Resort

👁 www.daydream.net.au

✆ 1800 075 040

Development Bureau of Hinchinbrook & Cardwell Shires

👁 www.hinchinbrookferries.com.au

✆ (07) 4776 5381

Dunk Island Resort

👁 www.dunkislandresort.com

✉ visitors@greatbarrierreef.aus.net

✆ (07) 4068 8199

Fitzroy Island Resort

👁 www.great-barrier-reef.com/fitzroy

✆ 1800 079 080

Great Barrier Reef Visitors Bureau

👁 www.greatbarrierreef.aus.net

✉ visitors@greatbarrierreef.aus.net

✆ (07) 4099 4644

Great Barrier Reef Marine Park Authority

👁 www.gbrmpa.gov.au

✆ (07) 4750 0700

Great Keppel Island Resort

👁 www.mpx.com.au/~adventures/gk/keppel.htm

✆ (07) 4939 5044

Green Island Resort

👁 www.greenislandresort.com.au

✉ res@greenislandresort.com.au

✆ (07) 4031 3300

Internet Info

Hamilton Island Resort

👁www.hamiltonisland.com.au

✆1800 075 110

Hayman Island Resort

👁www.hayman.com.au

✆(07) 4946 1234

Heron Island Resort

👁www.heronisland.com

✉visitors@greatbarrierreef.aus.net

✆132 469.

Hook Island Resort

👁www.hookislandresort.com.au

✉enquiries@hookis.com

✆(07) 4946 9380

Lady Elliot Island

👁www.ladyelliot.com.au

✉info@ladyelliot.com.au

✆1800 072 200

Lizard Island Resort

👁www.lizardislandresort.com

✉visitors@greatbarrierreef.net.au

✆(07) 4060 3999

Mackay Tourism and Development Bureau

✉mtdb@mackay.net.au

✆(07) 4952 2677,

Magnetic Island Tourist Information Bureau

👁www.magnetic-island.com.au

✆(07) 4778 5596

Mission Beach Visitor Information Centre

✉visitors@znet.net.au

✆(07) 4068 7066

Orpheus Island Resort

👁www.orpheusisland.com

✉reserv@greatbarrierreef.aus.net

✆(07) 4777 7377

Port Douglas Tourist Information Centre

👁www.portdouglas.com

✉reserv@greatbarrierreef.aus.net

✆(07) 4099 5599

South Molle Island Resort

👁www.southmolleisland.com.au

✉info@southmolleisland.com.au

✆(07) 4946 9433

Tourism Tropical North Queensland

👁www.tnq.org.au

✉ttnq@tnq.org.au

✆(07) 4051 3588

Trinity Beach

👁www.trinitybeach.com

✉info@trinitybeach.com

Tropical Tableland Promotion Bureau

👁www.athertontableland.com

✉info@athertontableland.com

✆4091 4222

Whitsunday Visitors and Convention Bureau

👁www.whitsundayinformation.com.au

or 👁www.whitsunday.net.au

✉tw@whitsundayinformation.com.au

✆(07) 4946 6673

Yorkeys Knob

👁www.yorkeysknob.com

✉hmbr@internetnorth.com.au

INDEX

Index

OTHER TRAVEL TITLES FROM LITTLE HILLS PRESS

Prices listed are recommended retail only, include GST and were correct at time of printing.

AUSTRALIAN TITLES

1863151524	Doing the Coast: Great Stay Guide	$21.95
1863151125	Outback Australia	$21.95
1863151095	Small Hotels of Sydney	$9.95
1863151451	Sydney: Short Stay Guide	$16.95
1863151419	Tasmania: Short Stay Guide	$18.95

Australian Pocket Guidebooks

1863150900	Melbourne	$5.95
186315101X	Brisbane & Gold/Sunshine Coasts	$13.95

Australian Driving Guides

1863150617	Australia's Central & Western Outback	$9.95
1863151109	Australia's Eastern Outback	$9.95
1863151338	Australia's South East	$19.95
1863151109	Australia's Wet Tropics & North-Eastern Outback	$9.95
1863151303	Outback Western Queensland	$9.95

OVERSEAS TITLES

1863151192	California	$19.95
186315132X	Cambodia: Short Stay Guide	$18.95
186315129X	Fiji	$9.95
1863151478	Hong Kong & Macau: Short Stay Guide	$16.95
1863150552	London Pocket Guidebook	$6.50
1863151141	New Zealand	$19.95
1863151265	Singapore	$9.95
1863150455	Singapore Pocket Guidebook	$6.50
1863150889	South Korea	$19.95
1863151036	South Pacific Islands	$19.95
1863151184	Thailand	$19.95

OTHER

1863151044	Travel Diary	$18.65

LITTLE HILLS PRESS ORDER FORM

Your details:

Name:_____

Address (of delivery):

_____

_____

Phone Number:_____

Email:_____

ISBN	TITLE	PRICE	QTY	TOTAL
_____	_____	_____	_____	_____
_____	_____	_____	_____	_____
_____	_____	_____	_____	_____
_____	_____	_____	_____	_____
_____	_____	_____	_____	_____
_____	_____	_____	_____	_____
_____	_____	_____	_____	_____

TOTAL BOOKS*_____

TOTAL PRICE*_____

How To Order

By Fax: 61 2 9838 7929

By Post: 3/18 Bearing Road, Seven Hills NSW 2147 Sydney, Australia

By Email: ✒info@littlehills.com

👁www.littlehills.com

*An additional freight charge applies to orders containing less than 5 books in total and orders to be sent outside Australia